# Power Up for the God Challenge: The Battle to Receive Your Real Man

Nicole Showell, M.A.

The Showell Foundation, Inc.

First published by Dog Ear Publishing
4011 Vincennes Rd
Indianapolis, IN 46268
www.dogearpublishing.net

ISBN: 978-1-4575-5380-6

This book is printed on acid-free paper.

Printed in the United States of America

I dedicate this book to CPS. I love you.

# Acknowledgments

Thank You, Jesus! What an awesome privilege to scribe a book directed by You to bless folk! I am extremely grateful for the opportunity to serve. I had so many encouragers along the way. Thanks to all of you so very much for your love and support. None were greater than Alicia Teet ... thanks so much for being there *every* step of the way! Reggie Walters ... what can I say ... your words of encouragement gave me strength and your advice was immeasurable. I thank God for my pastor, Bishop Walter S. Thomas; your loving spirit and weekly words have helped me become the woman of God I am today ... a woman who desires to be better and do better. Sincere and special thank-yous to Mommy for always being *the* support system, to Angela for encouragement that made me more determined, and to Indica for helping me stay up nights to finish the book (wink). Daddy, rest in peace; you were a real man, and I thank you for setting that example for me.

I thank the Showell Foundation Board of Directors; I appreciate that you appreciate this vision. Last but not least, my sweetest and dearest Chelsea; thank you for the drive to get up early and go to bed late. It is most important to me that I set a positive and loving example through word and action in everything I do, and it blesses me more than you will ever know to see you emulate that love. I am so proud of you, and I promise to always make you proud. You are my favorite, and I love you so much.

With all my love,

Nicole

# Table of Contents

*G*od wants the best for you, and I therefore want you to be the best you can be. When you know and commit to Jesus, you find that you want the best for every one of His children because that is the love He has placed within. Love knows only how to lift up and make better; it does not condemn or tear down. God created you in His image. You are like God; you have His blood flowing through your veins, His character traits, and His power! You are not made in the image of societal norms such as your job, wealth, and socioeconomic status. These norms do not define who you are or what you are capable of becoming, in relationships or otherwise. God does. He, and He alone, knows everything about you: with whom you are meant to spend your life, if you will be obedient and settle down with the one He destined for you, and if you will reject Him and follow your own desires.

This book was written with a pure heart and with the intention to help you be the woman God wants you to be in the relationship He wants you to have. He wants you to be wise and to be able to discern what is of Him and what is of the adversary. God wants to see you prosper and blessed in the relationship He has for you, not to fall into the traps that satan[1] has strategically laid for you. Being wise and discerning means rebuking societal norms that dictate your response to and within relationships, knowing what God wants for you in a relationship, being able to identify who was sent by God and who was sent by satan, being cognizant of what your godly role and responsibilities are and are not in relationships, and knowing how to handle sensitive and challenging topics that arise.

Wisdom affords you the insight to know that a man having a nice car, big house, and monetary wealth does not necessarily mean he is for you. It does, however, mean that you are so in tune with God's spirit that you can discern who God has delivered into your life to bless you and who satan brought to bring you down. Such wisdom solidifies your ability to make decisions based on truth, not on the deceptions of the world. Have you ever made one of the following statements?

- I will wait until I am established in my career before I settle down and get married.

- I will wait until I have enough saved in the bank before I start a relationship; just in case this marriage does not work out, I need to be prepared.

---

[1] The lowercase spelling of *satan* is not a typographical error but is because of my personal preference to not capitalize the name.

- I will wait until I lose 30 pounds before I consider a relationship.

- My boyfriend says we cannot move forward with our relationship until he gets the promotion at work.

- My fiancé says to push back the wedding until he buys the new house.

- Even though my boyfriend and I have been dating for seven years, he has to accomplish certain milestones on his own before we get married.

Are these statements made by you or God? He is the God of abundance, overflow, and perfection, and when He says it is time to move forward with a relationship, wisdom allows you to recognize that and to respond accordingly. It is important to understand that God does not order our steps based on *our* determination of readiness. I pray this book sheds His light and opens the door for the wisdom given to you by Him to guide your relational decisions.

In relationships, both men and women often base their actions on the societal norm of walking by sight rather than by faith, but God is telling you that it is time to switch and walk by faith, not by sight (2 Corinthians 5:7)[2]. If you walk by faith rather than by sight, you will eliminate a lot of unnecessary drama and hurt, and more of your focus will be on God rather than on the world. This book will bring you closer to God's plan for your life and help you build a solid foundation to support the relationship He wants you to have with the man He has destined for you. Does a relationship determined by the Father look like abuse? Cheating? Lies?

What does your heart say? If your answer is "yes" to any of these, I pray that during the course of reading this book, you will come to know that He wants only the best for you, and His best includes all things love. Cheating, lies, and abuse are contrary to everything God is and are not of Him. As He reveals His loving spirit and you receive a true sense of who He is, you will know what is and is not of Him in your relationship.

The first few chapters of this book reveal certain ugly truths about the "boys" you may typically date, so you may begin to understand the difference between boys and men and that God wants you to be with a real man. We will then transition into how the wisdom of God will guide you into making decisions that support His will for your life and lead you to a divinely prepared relationship with a man of God. It is time to be wise and make wise decisions.

---

[2] All Scripture referenced is from the NIV version unless otherwise noted.

Men and women with relational trials and challenges come to me as a professional counselor and mental health clinician for support and healing, to regain trust, and to better understand each other. I have counseled people from all walks of life … young, mature, professional athletes, corporate executives, educated, uneducated, laypeople, entrepreneurs, and more. People often ask me relationship questions because they desire to strengthen their relationships and to understand each other, though they may not know how. People want to be better and to do better for themselves and for their significant others but often find they are stuck in the world and cannot seem to get beyond what society dictates as relationally correct.

The Lord gave me the vision to write this book because He wants women to know exactly what relationships with real men look like and how to identify what is and is not godly in a relationship. It is important that you be able to identify the red flags when they are waved and that you have the strength to act accordingly to remove yourself from unhealthy or unsafe relationships. God is the God of love, safety, and security, and He wants that for you always as His daughter. Our Father wants you to be aware of the types of boys the adversary sends your way to distract you from walking according to His plan. This allows you to tell that adversary, "You gotta go," because it is time to get powered up and be blessed! God wants you to know that you are truly cherished and He treasures you so much that He gave His only Son for you. He desires for you to have a real man in your life, one who strives daily to live in a Christlike way and to do better and be better. It is important to recognize your value and to not settle for the boys that play games and regularly hurt you or cause distress.

Ups and downs in healthy and safe relationships are normal, but the way we experience and deal with them is extremely important to God and should be to you too. After reading this book, you will be able to identify which ups and downs are healthy rather than unhealthy, as well as helpful options for facing these challenges. Accommodating the games men play in an effort to have a healthy relationship is simply not healthy. It is time for men to step up and be men and for you to enjoy and be blessed by a *real* man! It is time to change the flawed perception of what a man is, and it is time to put God's values first and let Him show you the right man. Get ready to receive the man God called you to have!

I have spoken with men and women who have been on both sides of infidelity—failed relationships that they once anticipated would lead them down the aisle of marriage—and their share of games. In the majority of my clients and through the many conversations I have had with people, I see a common theme amongst relational challenges: The men enjoy having the stability of "good" women in their lives but still find themselves in scenarios that lead to inappropriate behavior, and the women attempt to accommodate the needs of their men and to work through the relational challenges they have. This is not the case in every relationship but in the majority of them of the individuals I counsel.

Before my daddy died in 2012, he would regularly say, "I feel sorry for women who are single these days." He was referencing how difficult it was to find a real, good man—one who would be honest, faithful, a good steward; put the needs of his family first; be a provider; and love the Lord.

In the book *Act Like a Lady, Think Like a Man*, author Steve Harvey wrote, "I want every woman who truly wants a solid relationship but just can't figure out how to get one, and those who are already in a relationship and trying to figure out how to make it better, to forget everything she's ever been taught about men—erase the myths, the heresy, everything your mother told you, everything your girlfriends told you, all the advice you've read in magazines and seen on television—and find out here, in these pages, who men really are." If it is of a carnal nature, then yes, it is beneficial to forget what you have read in magazines and seen on television. Most often, those images and messages are not in line with what God says a relationship is and should be. However, in some woman-to-woman conversations there is wisdom and truth that can be received, as long as the speaker is speaking from a godly perspective. Listen to these women with open ears and an open heart, because they know that of which they speak. Receiving wisdom and being able to discern what is and is not of God is crucial in receiving the man God has prepared for you in a healthy relationship and in not being fooled by the carnal man speaking untruths. Wisdom is a gift from God and comes only from God, so wise counsel from any godly woman should be warmly received.

"Blessed are those who find wisdom [blessed are those who find God], those who gain understanding for she is more profitable than silver and yields better returns than gold." —Proverbs 3:13-14 NIV

"[Wisdom] is a tree of life to those who take hold of her; those who hold her fast will be blessed." —Proverbs 3:18

"My son, do not let wisdom out of your sight, preserve sound judgment and discretion." —Proverbs 3:21

*Power up* is for every woman who desires a healthy relationship and wants her relationship to be based on the solid foundation of God and His wisdom, love, and truth. It can be a challenge to live the life God has called you to live and to be the woman He has called you to be because of the surrounding worldly influences that constantly reject God's Word. It is also a battle to overcome the worldly influences and the adversarial temptations that encourage your spiritual demise. You have to fight and stay powered up on His Word, through prayer, and by having an intimate relationship with God.

This book will help you steer clear of the games that prevent you or hinder your ability to have a successful relationship. You will understand the dynamics and importance of living a life that pleases our Father, thereby pleasing yourself and your mate, and receiving all that God has for you. It is my sincere prayer that you will be inspired to love with the love of Jesus in your relationship and prepare yourself to receive that same love while sharing the love of Jesus with everyone you know. God desires the best for you and your significant other, and this book is a great first step in establishing a healthy foundation for you and your mate.

*Power up for the God Challenge: The Battle to Receive Your Real Man* will ignite a greater understanding of relationships in you based on the word of God, not the carnality of the world, and will serve as a guide to God's plan for you and your relationship.

# I: WHAT'S IN HIS WALLET?

Men carry cards in their wallet; it is important to determine which card your man, or potential man, is carrying. Contrary to popular belief, most males carry a boy card, though they attempt to flaunt the man card. This reminds me of a scene from the movie *Sprung* in which Joe Torry, on his way to a party, stops by an ATM in a borrowed Porsche. He is looking for a bank receipt showing a five-digit balance so he can impress and pick up women at a party.

Much like Joe's character, worldly men attempt to flash a card they have not yet been able to acquire. So I ask you, "What is in his wallet?" Is it the man card or a boy card?

This section looks at the four boy cards that are most frequently carried:

- The Pretender

- The Bully

- The Coward

- The User

Note: When I refer to some males as boys instead of men, it is in no way to condemn but to help differentiate between the two. God has established certain criteria that define what a man is, and any male who does not meet this criteria, I therefore refer to as a boy.

# 1.

# THE PRETENDER

*Yet they shamelessly cheat widows out of their property and then pretend to be pious by making long prayers in public. Because of this, they will be more severely punished.*

—Luke 20:47 (NLT)

*W*e begin with a couple I previously counseled, Nancy and Keith.[3] I will refer to them throughout the book because of their relational dynamics and the insight offered by their relationship.

Keith had the smoothest silver tongue Nancy had ever encountered. He could talk his way into getting whatever he wanted and could get out of any situation. He charmed his way into her life with tall tales of commitment and security. He knew who he was and what he wanted to do with his life, and he was working his plan to ensure that his future would be bright and he would be successful (based on the world's definition of success). He painted a beautiful picture of them together in the future. He was motivated and action-oriented. He was contrary to the guys she had dated in the past. Keith was much younger than her (eight years), was not financially affluent, and was not as intellectually stimulating as the men she normally dated, but he had street smarts and intrigued Nancy. She wanted to find out more about him and was encouraged to do so by a dear friend of hers because he was different and different can be great!

Nancy quickly met Keith's family, including his mother, grandmother, sisters, and brothers. He met her family and friends. Shortly after they started dating, he asked her to move in with him. She had never lived with a man before, but after thinking it over for a couple of days, she excitedly said yes. They had fun and made each other laugh and seemed to be a great fit. Because Nancy's job allowed for more flexibility than Keith's traditional 9–5, she was able to maintain a clean apartment, fold and put away the laundry, make sure he had a hot meal when he came home from work, take him to the train station in the morning

All names and some identifying details have been changed to protect the privacy of individuals.

and pick him up in the afternoon, and make sure that he and the house had everything they needed. Everything was great.

Until she started noticing little things here and there that did not make sense. (Ladies, when what you see and what he says do not match, it is normally because something slippery is going on.) For example, he always stated that he kept work strictly professional and did not fraternize with anyone at work, but he regularly texted a girl from work. He would tell Nancy that he was not interested in any other women and that he did not speak to other women on the phone. Despite telling her this, he invited a former girlfriend to visit him when he went to Miami during a holiday weekend with the boys, and he returned from Miami with new telephone numbers in his phone. When Nancy inquired about the inconsistencies, he had a quick response for each circumstance and proclaimed his integrity.

 **Red Flag**: *Ladies, when what you see and what he says don't match, it is because something not quite right is going on.*

Nancy learned the hard way that Keith carried a boy card in his wallet but that if she hadn't come to know the real him, she would have still thought that he had a long and positive credit history with the man card. Keith falls into the category of the Pretender.

The root of a boy pretending to be a man is lack of faith. Though Keith walked and talked as a man of faith, his heart and actions were far removed from being those of a faith-filled man of God.

The Pretender leads a woman down a path while she is wearing the rose-colored glasses he gave her. Let's discuss some of the characteristics of a Pretender.

## Appears Too Good to Be True

Women have an instinctual desire to be with men who seem to have it all: sense of humor, sexual skill, sturdy goals and aspirations, motivation, ability to amass wealth, strong sense of family, strong character and integrity, honesty, education, ability to provide, handiness, and love of the Lord. (Men have an instinctual desire to be with women who are nurturing, make a house a home, are supportive, are freaks in bed and ladies in public, and confess to love the Lord. Quite a different list!) These are the things that most women want, and if a woman meets someone who is able to impress upon her that he is all of these things, she believes she has hit the jackpot!

Things are not always what they appear, however, though sometimes they are. It is up to you to utilize discernment and wisdom to make the determination. If he appears too good to be true and has no actions to back up the appearance, he probably *is* too good to be true. If he attempts to make you believe that he is all of these things by simply saying he is, it should raise a red flag; however, if he actively demonstrates through consistent and persistent action that he is a man of God who loves, is compassionate and kind, puts you first, and is not self-seeking, he is, more than likely, authentic.

Nancy and Keith went through the ups and downs and downs again of their relationship. He started off as someone who appeared too good to be true, and unfortunately for Nancy, he was. He confessed his love for Jesus and that he lived for Him. He admitted that he had not always treated women right in relationships, but he tried to convince Nancy that the past was behind him and he wanted her to be his one and only. He confided that he was going to build a family with Nancy and he was going to work hard to make sure his family was taken care of. He spent a significant amount of time volunteering at his church and wanted to see young people excel in life. He made sure that Nancy was aware of this side of him, and he expertly shielded her from the boy beneath this seemingly perfect man.

Nancy later found out that she was not the only one in his life and that he regularly added women to his entourage. Further, he embellished his relationship with Jesus and did not believe or follow His precepts as he had indicated. She also learned that part of his desire was to attach himself to her because she had a lot to offer: she was actively supportive of him and his goals, was financially established, and provided the nurturing and loving environment that most men want. Only after she had become completely enthralled by him did she realize that it was all an act; by then, they had moved in together and were planning for a family.

## Has a Quick and Witty Response to All Inquiries That Challenge His Integrity

When caught in an untruth or inappropriate behavior, a Pretender's first reaction is to become defensive. Then he will create and share a lie that he hopes will get you to move on without additional questions being asked. Most women will not lose trust in their men unless they have solid evidence. When the boy responds in a way that does not make sense, a woman will continue to ask questions until she is satisfied that he is not being dishonest and convinced that what he is saying is true.

After having observed Nancy and Keith for several months, I saw that he regularly displayed immediate agitation when she questioned anything he did that was out of character for a godly man. The things she questioned were behaviors or events that he had engaged in or acted upon that he was hoping to keep hidden from her. For example, when she asked him about the text conversations with his female coworker whom he had previously denied communicating with, he stated that the coworker was going through a rough time and he was trying to be a friend to her. Keith forcefully exclaimed that there was nothing between them and that he was just encouraging her through a life challenge. What Nancy did not yet know was that Keith being a friend to his coworker included having sex with her and them taking pornographic pictures of each other.

## Acts Differently, but Better, When People Are Around

The Pretender wears many hats and is a different person in front of his boss, mother, father, church family, and so on. In a relationship, the woman eventually sees the *real* person, who he really is and not who he presents himself as to the rest of the world. The friendly, patient, honest, empathetic, calm, and above-reproach guy she sees at church, work, or with the family is not the same guy who lies next to her. But why not? The guy that his coworkers love and family adores can and should be the same for her, but there is something almost instinctual in him that says, "Let me be the boy to the woman who does everything for me. Though she is supportive and loving, does so much for me—including encouraging me and supporting my dreams, doing the laundry, cooking my meals, and taking care of the house—I am going to lie to her, cheat on her, physically abuse her, or cause mental and emotional suffering. I'll demonstrate that I am a man at work, in church, and with my family, but with her, I'll be the boy."

A former associate of mine, Haley, was in an abusive relationship, but no one on the outside would have ever thought that her boyfriend, Tom, had a problem controlling his anger. When I met Tom, he was the epitome of a gentleman. He treated Haley well, talked to her sweetly, and protected her as if she were the First Lady of the United States and he was a Secret Service agent. Again, however, things are not always as they appear. If not for Haley's busted lip and bruised face, I would have never believed that Tom was beating her.

Haley defended Tom in the worst way. (I say *worst* because though she defended him tirelessly, it was a painful and unhealthy stance to take.) It is very true that when you are in a relationship, it is hard to see what is going on. Publicly, Tom appeared to be a man of noble character and openly shared that Haley was the love of his life and he wanted to spend his life protecting and providing for her.

Privately, however, his actions were contrary to his public displays of affection. At home, he berated her for not completing housework quickly enough or for wanting to spend time with friends. Haley felt amazing when she was out with him but had an internal struggle about how the private face she saw of him was different from that public face.

## Speaks One Way but Acts Another

This is a very big area where women must be very attentive. Boys say a lot of things that their actions do not match. This is commonplace among boys, and women seem to let it slide as long as their men are whispering sweet nothings and providing the seemingly important relational components.

You can learn a lot by what a guy says versus what he does. For example, him saying, "I love you" does not match with the behavior of physically violating a woman or causing her mental or emotional suffering. "I love you" does not look like inappropriate and explicit text messages or e-mails that support cheating or lying. "I want to spend the rest of my life with you" does not look like adding new telephone numbers from other women to his phone and denying that he has a girlfriend, fiancée, or wife.

Tina, a 24-year-old client who seeks regular relational counsel, is a young woman with the world at her fingertips. She is bright and beautiful but regularly chose to overlook the mixed messages she received from her soon-to-be ex-husband and her potential future husband. Her soon-to-be ex-husband frequently cheated, lied, privately humiliated her, and called her everything but a child of God, but seconds later said, "I love you."

He tried to have sex with his sister-in-law and with Tina's best friend. Tina gave him a healthy and beautiful baby girl, and he posted messages on Facebook about having sex with his girlfriends. His way of honoring the mother of his child was to go overseas and have sex with various women he met in port and to post pictures of them on his Facebook page. I regularly asked Tina if what her husband said matched his actions: When he said he was going to do right, did his Facebook photos of the ladies he had recently been with support what he said? Did removing all of the money from the bank account and leaving Tina without a penny to take care of her daughter show the love he said he had for her? He was a Pretender who appeared to be a loving husband who put his family first, but really made himself the priority over both mother and child. His actions and words did not match.

When your significant other makes himself the priority in the relationship, you will rarely find that his actions match his words, because the focus is on him instead of you.

Tina's potential future husband, Jeremy, whom she had been dating for nine months, said wonderful things, but his actions were mediocre at best. One thing that I appreciate in *Act Like a Lady, Think Like a Man* is that the author recognizes that when a couple are married or in a relationship that is going to lead to marriage, the male in should no longer have friends who are women. The man should no longer regularly communicate with his exes or with women he has dated, and neither should the woman. If the couple, collectively, is not friends with a person, that friendship should not exist.

Jeremy continued to be friends with his ex-girlfriend Sarah, against Tina's wishes. Though Tina had made him aware of her concerns, he did not respect that she was uncomfortable that Sarah still came to his home and also went out for dinner and drinks with him. Jeremy posted pictures on social media of his outings with Sarah, and all the while, Tina was upset and internally questioned his love for and dedication to her.

One night, Jeremy, Tina, and Sarah were all at Jeremy's parents' home and he and Sarah both disappeared for several minutes. Tina could not find him anywhere. She looked throughout the house, from the basement to the third floor, without any luck. She then took her search outside and after several minutes saw a car speeding down the cul-de-sac and Jeremy emerging from the darkness into the light outside of the house. Tina asked him where he had been, and his response was, "I was just walking Sarah to the car." Though there were several people enjoying the festivities at his parents' home, he had made the poor decision to take 15–20 minutes to walk Sarah to the car instead of asking another of their mutual friends to do it.

Tina was torn between the random words of kindness of her soon-to-be ex-husband and the sweet oratory of her potential future husband, but neither of them have actions and commentary that coincide.

## Does Not Maintain His Pre-Relationship Performance in the Relationship

I have heard many times in the confidential comforts of a counseling session, and experienced for myself, the woes of pre-relationship performance demise. Initially, the Pretender works hard to get a woman by pulling out all the stops: romance, chivalry, and the platinum rule (treating others as *they* want to be treated). It is as if a core, but subliminal, component to his psyche says, "I will do this until she is mine, and then I will stop and revert to the real me. I will create a façade and present a captivating performance for as long as it takes, and once she is completely attached, I will show the real me and the repeat performances will be finished." His expectations of you remain intact, however.

For example, he expects you to maintain your looks (hair, figure, wardrobe, etc.) and to continue to represent him well—which, of course, you should do for yourself and because you represent God daily. If you are unsuccessful, it could create a relational challenge that validates his motives for seeking extracurricular activities. As a child of God, you deserve the very best, and if he is unwilling to provide his best, which the Bible says he should, or if his best is only temporary, it is confirmation that he has not yet become the man God intended.

"Whatever you do, work at it with all your heart, as working for the Lord, not for human masters, since you know that you will receive an inheritance from the Lord as a reward. It is the Lord Christ you are serving" (Colossians 3:23–24). Whatever you do, whether in word or deed, do it all in the Name of the Lord Jesus, giving thanks to God the Father through Him. Giving thanks to God is a key part of this Scripture. When God allows people into your life, that blessing He provides is followed by praise and thanksgiving. When someone is thankful for someone or something, they treat it very well. As such, your man should regularly demonstrate that he is thankful for you. (We will explore what this looks like coming chapters.)

I spoke with a couple having marital challenges due to the husband's infidelity. They had dated in college, gotten engaged after graduation, and been married a few months later. From the moment he had met her, he knew he wanted her to be his wife. After months of doing everything necessary to get and keep her attention and to plant himself in her life, however, he reverted to his ways of womanizing and had affairs with other women. The man he had worked so hard to present as honest and noble was diametric to his reality as he returned to being a lover to many.

## Says His Life Is an Open Book and Invites You to Know It All but Does Not Share Openly

The Pretender hides a lot and shares only what he wants his woman to know, and only half of what he shares is accurate. Not every person is going to tell his or her partner 100 percent of everything, but it is important that you be with a man who understands the importance of starting and maintaining a relationship with integrity and with open and honest communication. Any relationship that begins with deceit will inevitably fail. I will be the first to admit that it is not always easy to decipher lies from truth, and this is exactly why it is extremely important to watch a man's actions and see if they are aligned with what he says.

Amber and Josh had known each other for years before they started dating. Before they became a serious couple, they had honest, lengthy, and intense discussions about relationships. When the opportunity presented itself for a relationship, Amber was ready to move forward with Josh. She quickly learned, however, that their "honest" talks were not an accurate depiction of Josh. Amber did not realize that during these pre-relationship talks, Josh had already planned that he was going to date her and utilized that opportunity to engage her.

During sessions, Josh regularly stated, "Honesty is extremely important in our relationship, and if you lie to me, I'm out. If you cheat on me, I'm out … so don't ever do it." Amber thought he was genuine, and she never had any intention of cheating on or lying to him; she also inferred that he would never do these things to her. This is what I like to call the flip trick. The Pretender will put what he is doing on you and make you cognizant that the type of behavior mentioned is unacceptable, thereby encouraging you to believe that it is something he would never do. While he is telling you this, he is engaged in the deviant behavior that he says is unacceptable. He wants you to believe that he is a man of integrity so you will accept everything he tells you as truth.

I know women want more than anything to have confidence in our men, to have faith in what they say, and for them to be the men they claim they are, but we must be wise and discerning and listen to our heavenly Father. I used to always say that if I saw questionable behavior early in a relationship, I would not stick around to see more of the same. I never thought of myself as one of those women who stays with someone in the hope that I would change him, because if he was showing me crazy now, he would definitely show me elevated levels of crazy later. But I learned that never is a long time.

 **QUICK FACT:**

Guys know their limitations and their strengths but can make their limitations look like their greatest assets. They do this because of you; they want you. They see something that they want to have and can play the game accordingly. It is important to identify what is a façade and what is authentic.

## Helpful Scriptures

"All you need to say is simply 'Yes' or 'No'; anything beyond this comes from the evil one." (Matthew 5:37)

"But the noble make noble plans, and by noble deeds they stand. You women who are so complacent, rise up and listen to me; you daughters who feel secure, hear what I have to say!" (Isaiah 32:8–9)

"We are careful to be honorable before the Lord, but we also want everyone else to see that we are honorable." (2 Corinthians 8:21 NLT)

## Activity

After reading the Pretender section, do you feel that you are currently dating or have previously dated a Pretender? If so, how do you, or did you, feel about his role in your relationship and in your life?

---

---

---

---

---

In your relationship, do you pay attention to whether your man's comments are aligned with his actions? If not, why? Do you feel it is important that his words and actions be aligned?

---

---

---

---

---

What can you do, moving forward, that will prevent you from dating someone with the Pretender card?

_____

_____

_____

_____

_____

## Prayer

 Father, I come to You giving thanks for who You are and for Your amazing goodness. The traits of a Pretender seem all too familiar, and I thank You for revealing things that I should be cognizant of and should observe in my relationship. Today, I am going to seek You first as I take the first steps in learning more about You and what You want for me in my relationship. I know it is not someone who pretends to be something he is not! Open my heart and eyes to discern what is a trap of the adversary; help me to make decisions based on the spirit and not the world as I move forward in my relationship. I need Your help. I admit I cannot do it on my own, but with You, I can do anything. I love You and thank You for leading and guiding me in my relationship. In Jesus' name I pray. Amen.

# 2

# THE BULLY

*In the day when I cried out, You answered me, and made me bold with strength in my soul.*

—Psalm 138:3

*W*hen women think of the term *bully* regarding relationships, the most common thought is of physical intimidation. In this chapter, we will see that bullying extends beyond the physical realm and into the mental, emotional, and even spiritual realms. Insecurity is the main characteristic of the Bully type. The Bully gets pleasure from placing you in a position of submission. His goal is to appear powerful to make you feel powerless. His insecurity issues are coupled with low self-esteem, which means he wants to strip you of your dignity and self-esteem as well. You will notice that the Bully not only sacrifices your self-esteem but may also inflict physical, verbal, emotional, mental, and spiritual abuse. Just like the other types of boys, the Bully does not fully trust God or have complete faith in Him; as such, he does not know who he is in God and is thus unable to love you with the love of Jesus. If you are in a relationship with a Bully, he may say he loves you and that his bullying is often a mistake that will not happen again, but you may find that the mistake happens regularly anyway.

In 2014, an argument caught on camera and leaked to the media showed a man punching his girlfriend with such intensity that he knocked her unconscious. As with the Pretender, the majority of the Bully's family members and coworkers have no idea that he is a bully. They believe he is the person he presents to them, and most are shocked when they find out otherwise. For example, several interviews were conducted with the filmed man's acquaintances following the incident, but one in particular caught my attention. An interviewer asked the father of the victim if the Bully had ever demonstrated bully-like behavior. The father responded that the guy was good one and he had not seen any bully tendencies in him. The victim's father continued to say that if something had been awry, intervention would have been necessary, but everything had seemed perfect.

It can be hard to recognize the Bully in a relationship, especially if the Bully tries to keep it a secret. The appearance of a perfect relationship is normally a strong indicator that things are not, in fact, perfect. Nothing is ever perfect in any relationship or with any individual. We try to be better and do better and to be the people God has called us to be, but we will fall short, which is okay, as long as we are making efforts to be better.

Just like the Pretender has the uncanny ability to distract people from whom he is at his core and to persuade people to believe the façade he presents as authentic, so the Bully must also keep up appearances as a protective and honorable man. When the scary and disturbing videos were released of the Bully punching out his girlfriend, my initial professional opinion was that the woman involved, a beloved daughter of the Most High, had probably experienced this horrific interaction before. While following the story, I saw a few things that offered support to my initial opinion:

- The victim's family was more distraught when addressing the strangers who talked badly about the victim than when discussing the assault.

- The ease in which they had the physical altercation, alcohol or not, had the appearance that it was not new to either of them.

- The tone of the Bully's preliminary apologies and his later apologies were starkly different. In the initial televised apologies, he appeared to be extremely remorseful, with his girlfriend being the priority, but in later apologies, he appeared to consider her only as an afterthought, giving little or no concern to her mental or emotional state.

I have no question that the man gave his girlfriend heartfelt apologies in private, but I believe that no matter how many times someone apologizes, or the context of the apology, every apology should be said with authenticity and passionate remorse. When Keith apologized to Nancy, for example, the first couple of times appeared heartfelt and remorseful with tears. After that, however, his apologies became angry and resentful. He was tired of her lingering tears, flashbacks, and brokenness. When a man of God wrongs someone, he will confess to that person and to God, but he will also be patient and loving after apologizing. If he gets to the point where he says he is sorry but his actions do not indicate that he means it, he should not say it. If the Bully has true repentance in his heart, he will be receptive to the pain that the other party is experiencing, will lovingly wait for that party's healing, and will acknowledge his role in the healing.

Www.stmonicaindy.org defines bullying as negative verbal or physical behavior that is done (1) directly to a person or person's property and (2) with the conscious intention of either upsetting the person or manipulating the person's behavior, and that (3) God would not approve of. I believe one of the most important components of this definition is that God would not approve. If you think about your significant other and ask yourself, "Would God approve of how he is treating me?" what would your response be? Allowing this simple but eye-opening question to be your standard will transform your thinking about relationships and what you will deem acceptable or intolerable. If you use God's approval as the benchmark, you will begin to see His desire for you and your relationship.

The Bible has several examples of bullying, but one that stands out for me is the bullying of Joseph, because he experienced it on multiple levels. Genesis 37 reveals that because Joseph was the favorite son to their father, Jacob, his brothers envied him. This envy created angst and troubled Joseph's relationship with his brothers so much that his brothers plotted to kill him. The oldest brother, Reuben, could not murder his brother, however, and suggested throwing Joseph into a pit instead. Joseph's brothers all agreed and stripped him of his colorful tunic, which had been a special gift from his father and symbolized his birthright. After Joseph's brothers threw him into the pit, a group of Ishmaelites (Ishmael was the son born of Abraham and his servant, Hagar) traveled across their path, and the brothers agreed to sell Joseph to them for twenty silver shekels. In turn, Joseph became a slave in Egypt. Joseph's brothers bullied him directly, taking away his freedom by forcing him into slavery and wresting away his birthright by taking his tunic.

The bullying of Joseph continues in Genesis 39. In Egypt, Joseph earned the trust of King Potiphar and became his right-hand man. Joseph faced intense bullying from his boss's wife, who desired Joseph sexually. Day after day, she flirted and made advances toward Joseph, and day after day, he rejected her. One day, she found herself alone with Joseph in the house and grabbed him. She was intent on having her way with him and told him to take her to bed! In an effort to remove himself from the precarious situation, Joseph ran out of the house, leaving his cloak in her clutch. Because he still would not return her advances, she made sure he was punished by falsely accusing him of trying to sexually assault her so the king threw him in jail.

---

**"You deserve love with someone who will cherish you as I [God] do."**

---

Keith, whom we've already met, was a multiple card carrier, the Bully card included. Keith's bullying was displayed through verbal, emotional, and physical violations. As soon as it became physical, Nancy did not stick around for additional abuse, however. She tolerated the verbal and emotional bullying because she believed that Keith would change, but when he showed her that he had no problem grabbing and punching her and pushing her into a wall, she realized that God wanted her out of the relationship. At that moment, she heard God speaking to her loud and clear: "I love you, and this is not what I, your Father, want for you. You deserve love with someone who will cherish you as I do." God did not approve of what she was experiencing. A man of God does not try to manipulate someone's behavior or treat someone poorly. A man of God makes every effort to protect, love, and show kindness; he wants to build up, not tear down. A man of God wants to strengthen, not weaken, his woman while they grow in Christ to become better together.

It was also at this moment that Nancy realized that everything Keith had ever promised to not doing to her, he had done—he had promised he would never lie, cheat, or hit her, and he had done all three. Had she been adorned with the wisdom she now has when she met him, Nancy certainly would not have subjected herself to such suffering at his hand, nor would she have ignored God's desires for her.

Keith made Nancy believe that they would always be together, that it was God's plan for them to be together. Manipulating behavior and making the woman believe that they are meant to be together are prime Bully tactics. Bullies will even add God into the scenario to make it wholly convincing. It worked on Nancy because she felt that if Keith referenced God, the things he said must be true.

Let's be clear here: Even the devil uses God's words against people to get them to do what he wants them to do. He used the Word of God to try to bully Jesus in Matthew 4:1–11:

> Then Jesus was led by the Spirit into the wilderness to be tempted by the devil. After fasting forty days and forty nights, he was hungry. The tempter came to him and said, "If you are the Son of God, tell these stones to become bread." Jesus answered, "It is written: 'Man shall not live on bread alone, but on every word that comes from the mouth of God.'" Then the devil took him to the holy city and had him stand on the highest point of the temple. "If you are the Son of God," he said, "throw yourself down. For it is written: 'He will command his angels concerning you, and they will lift you up in their hands, so that you

will not strike your foot against a stone.'" Jesus answered him, "It is also written: 'Do not put the Lord your God to the test.'" Again, the devil took him to a very high mountain and showed him all the kingdoms of the world and their splendor. "All this I will give you," he said, "if you will bow down and worship me." Jesus said to him, "Away from me, Satan! For it is written: 'Worship the Lord your God, and serve him only.'" Then the devil left him, and angels came and attended him.

This Scripture provides an excellent example of bullying. The devil attempted to bully Jesus by trying to manipulate His behavior, telling Him things that were untrue, and to get Jesus to do things that were contrary to what is righteous (God would not approve) and to God's Word. When you know God—really know Him—you are able to rebuke the lies of the devil. You can discern what is good and true and what is evil. You see in this Scripture that Jesus continuously replied with the Word of God and that the devil left. The devil saw that Jesus was strong in the Word and faithful, so his only recourse was to flee.

Here you have the devil, who knew that Jesus was feeling weak because He had not eaten in forty days. The devil offered Him the opportunity to turn stones to bread because Jesus had been without food for so long. The devil tried to get Jesus to engage in reckless behavior that would cause injury or death. Finally, he tried to tempt Jesus by offering Him great wealth and status, offering Him all the kingdoms of the world. This shows just how manipulative satan is; when offering Jesus the world, he was promising Him something that already belongs to Him. Because Jesus knew that the true riches of the world were of God and not of the world, He did not fall victim to the adversary.

This Scripture shows us that bullying is not just physical; the devil attempts to bully in the mental, emotional, and spiritual areas where people can be weakest. I think most people have experienced or can relate to the emotions that are tied to financial strain, the mental unrest of being hungry, or falling to our spiritual pride and being focused on doing something to prove our power to someone. Satan challenged Jesus in these areas, and he will also do so to you to get you to go against God's will.

It is also important to remember that satan bullied Jesus in a weak moment. Jesus had fasted for forty days and forty nights. When you go without food for that long, you lack your normal levels of physical, emotional, and mental strength and may succumb to just about any temptation for nourishment. Jesus had the Word of God rooted in His heart and drew His strength from that; God wants you to be the same way. This is why studying His Word, praying, praising, and worshipping are critical to your safety and success in removing yourself from a relationship with a bully.

Because the devil wants you to go against the Word of God, he may orchestrate meetings, entice you when you are weak, or purposely create scenarios so in which you feel weak, to cause you to neglect God's will in your life. Remember that you are strong in the Lord and that His power lives within you.

At the beginning of each new year, I spend three uninterrupted days with the Father to perform a spiritual review of the previous year. A few things I do during this time are pray, reflect on decisions I made, and plan what I need to do differently in the new year. I also look at the people in my life to determine if they helped or hindered me. In this time, I seek the Father and ask Him what He wants me to do and what changes I need to make.

Years ago, I dated someone who told me not to do my three-day spiritual review. He attempted to change my mind and to dissuade me from spending time with the Father because he wanted to spend time with me. I explained that it was important that I do this review every year. This man disagreed about the importance of enriching my relationship with the Lord and rebuked me and my desire to spend time with the Father. I did not realize it at the time, but this was spiritual bullying. I now believe he was in my life to try to get me to distance myself from the Lord and His will.

Have you ever been or are you now in a relationship with a bully?

Have you ever been

- told to do something that you know is contrary to the Word of God?

- told you were nothing?

- hit or pushed?

- spoken to in condescension or cursed out?

- told to do something you did not want to do?

- humiliated in front of friends, family, or colleagues?

- made to feel weak/helpless, or had your dignity damaged?

- forced by someone to do something to meet one of your emotional, mental, or physical needs?

If you answered yes to any of the above, you have experienced bullying. If you are regularly and consistently experiencing any of the above, you are in a relationship with a bully and it is time to be *bold with strength in your soul.* Fall down and pray, praise the Lord, stay strong in faith, discern with God-given wisdom what is of God and what is of the adversary, and use your weapon, the all-powerful Scripture, to repel the unwanted attacks against your spirit. Stand strong, believe in God, and trust that His Word is true. He wants you to end the cycle of bullying in your relationship and to no longer follow the deception of the world but, instead, to embrace and follow His steadfast Word. When you do not remain strong and are taken in by satan's silver tongue, you become victim to his bullying and he continues to bully.

Because you have God's power within, you are able to be strong and to stand against the intimidation of the Bully. Remember, the adversary can use anyone in his schemes and plots to bring you down, and if that person is the boy in your life, it is time to reevaluate and make a wise decision. Being strong in God's power does not mean staying in the relationship to take the bullying but means protecting yourself and honoring God by leaving a relationship that is working against your life and purpose. It is important to understand that your strength comes from God's Word; you have to enrich your relationship with Him by studying His Word and spending time with Him daily. Just as you try to enrich your relationship with your mate by spending time with and getting to know him, so must you do with your heavenly Father.

If you have fallen into the trap of the adversary and find yourself in a relationship with a Bully (or any other boy type) who does not have a desire to make godly changes in his life, it is time for you to make the godly decision to leave the relationship. Remember that you are loved and God wants only the best for you. He is not going to hold it against you that you were tricked by the adversary, and He certainly does not want you to beat yourself up about it. Jesus took the beating for you already. Instead of focusing on the past, look forward to what is ahead: a loving relationship when the time is right (the time has already been decided by God).

## Helpful Scriptures

"Finally, be strong in the Lord and in his mighty power. Put on the full armor of God, so that you can take your stand against the devil's schemes. For our struggle is not against flesh and blood, but against the rulers, against the authorities, against the powers of this dark world and against the spiritual forces of evil in the heavenly realms.

Therefore put on the full armor of God, so that when the day of evil comes, you may be able to stand your ground, and after you have done everything, to stand. Stand firm then, with the belt of truth buckled around your waist, with the breastplate of righteousness in place, and with your feet fitted with the readiness that comes from the gospel of peace. In addition to all this, take up the shield of faith, with which you can extinguish all the flaming arrows of the evil one. Take the helmet of salvation and the sword of the Spirit, which is the word of God. And pray in the Spirit on all occasions with all kinds of prayers and requests. With this in mind, be alert and always keep on praying for all the Lord's people." (Ephesians 6:10–18)

## Activity

I realize I am in a relationship with a Bully because I have experienced the following:

_____

_____

_____

_____

_____

I know God does not want me to continue in this relationship because:

_____

_____

_____

_____

_____

I am going to safely remove myself from this relationship by doing the following:

_____

_____

_____

_____

_____

Look in the mirror and say with strength, **"I am strong in the Lord! I have His power within! And with His power, I will be strong and courageous to bullying and intimidation! God loves me, and He wants me to be loved, so no longer, devil, will I be bullied!"**

Remember, when you decide to love yourself and honor God, pray for the words to share with your mate when it is time for you to leave the relationship. Pray for God's continued protection and safety as you follow His purpose for your life; He will open the doors for you to enjoy peace, joy, and the man He has destined for you. Stay in prayer as you follow His purpose for your life. You will be blessed!

## Prayer

God, You are a protector. You are my protector, and I know that You want me to be with a man who protects and defends me instead of bullying and hurting me. You want the best for me as Your child, and I want to do Your will. Please give me the wisdom I need to make Godlike decisions. Help me to stand firm in Your Word. I pray for the strength to resist the bullying and to live a life with the man You have destined to protect and love me! Love is patient and kind; it does no harm. I thank You for safely delivering me from a bullying relationship and preparing me to receive Your blessing: a man who is made in Your image, is wise and strong, and resists the temptations of the devil. He is also kind, patient, and has joy because he knows You, and we will help each other grow. Thank You for caring so much about me that You have freed me from the devil's trap and opened my eyes to see truth. I know that this is a process and I cannot do it by myself; I need You every step of the way. Not me Lord, but You. Help me to be strong and courageous, and guide me along the path of recognizing that I am and acting as a daughter of the Most High. Help me to love myself as You love me. I love you, Lord. In Jesus' name I pray. Amen.

# 3

# THE COWARD

*Be on your guard; stand firm in the faith; be (wo)men of courage; be strong. Do everything in love.*

—1 Corinthians 16:13–14

*T*he Coward lies because he is afraid to stand up and be a man. He is not capable of doing what he says, and he fills his lady's heart and ears with promises that he has no intention of keeping. The Coward wants to make his woman believe that he is a strong and take-charge man, but really, he lacks the courage to be the man he is called to be and professes to be. Unbeknownst to his woman, one of his main characteristics is fear but will never share that with her or anyone else because of his cowardice. Merriam-Webster[4] defines fear as "a painful emotion or passion excited by the *expectation of evil,* or the apprehension of impending danger; apprehension; anxiety; solicitude; alarm; dread. Fear is an *uneasiness of the mind,* upon the thought of future *evil* likely to befall us" (my emphasis). This definition is full of adversarial content and is contrary to everything that God is and that He desires for you: evil, the expectation of evil, and uneasiness of the mind. The devil is evil and desires for you to be uneasy and to experience the worst. Our Father, in contrast hand, longs for you to experience peace and joy, which are diametric to the fear that weighs down the Coward.

---

### We live in a world that encourages men to be boys in relationships.

---

The Bible gives several helpful Scriptures to provide insight on how to overcome cowardice. The Amplified version of John 12:42–43 reads, "And yet [in spite of all this] many even of the leading men (the authorities and the nobles) believed and trusted in Him. But because of the Pharisees they did not confess it, for fear that [if they should acknowledge Him] they would be expelled from the synagogue; for they loved the approval and the praise and the glory that come from

---

[4] All Merriam-Webster references cite the Merriam-Webster Collegiate Dictionary, Eleventh Edition, 2004.

men [instead of and] more than the glory that comes from God. [They valued their credit with men more than their credit with God]." Here, we learn that the Coward wants to fit in and not lose his worldly footing in the sight of those he looks up to, and that he seeks validation. He fears the outcome of doing what is good and right and rejects Jesus to follow the nefarious trends of his friends.

Does this sound like your guy? Do you find that he engages in behavior contrary to God because he opts to follow what is acceptable and normal in the world today? Not too many men take a public stand and defy society to do the right thing and honor God. You rarely see it in television or movies; you do not hear it often in music or observe it in music videos. You may only sometimes hear about it from your friends or read about it in the paper. Not many men are standing up and saying, "Treat your women right," and some of the ones who do, we later find out, are committing adultery, being physically abusive, or engaging in other duplicitous behavior. It is hypocrisy to publicly declare yourself a man who honors his lady while really carrying the Coward card or any other boy card. In Luke 16:15, Jesus says, "You are those who justify yourselves before men, but God knows your hearts. For what is exalted among men is an abomination in the sight of God" (ESV), and 1 Peter 2:1 reminds us "Therefore, rid yourselves of all malice and all deceit, hypocrisy, envy, and slander of every kind."

---

### The Coward lies because he is afraid to stand up and be a man.

---

When I think of the Coward, I remember the relationship between Amber and Josh. He was afraid of truly committing but wanted to make her believe with every inch of his being that he was ready and wanted a relationship with her. (Josh was actually a combination card carrier, but we will come back to that in Chapter 4.) A quote by Bob Marley sums it up nicely: "The biggest coward is a man who awakens a woman's love with no intention of loving her." At some point, most women will have this experience with such a man, because we live in a world that encourages men to be boys in relationships.

Josh and Amber went on a couple of dates while he was dating other women, and because he was not a fan of her abstaining from sex until she was married, he eventually started dating someone else exclusively. Because of his exclusivity, Josh cut off all communication with the other women he was dating, including Amber. Amber thought this was a noble action. Though she was disappointed they would not continue to get to know each other, she thought Josh's actions were upright.

After Josh's exclusive relationship ended, he called Amber from time to time over the span of two years but, for various reasons, she did not entertain his advances...until she reached out to him because she felt her season of abstention was coming to an end. She had an overwhelming desire to have sex. She phoned him to see if he wanted to hang out, though her true intention was to see if he could fill that void.

When the time came, Amber could not go through with having sex with Josh. Sex was still a meaningful and significant commitment for Amber, and her spirit would not allow her to have casual sex. She and Josh started having long discussions over lunch, however, and these became the highlight of her week. She was still healing from the emotional scars caused by her last boyfriend's infidelity and was very interested in hearing Josh's views on men and women, and on life in general. Josh opened up and gave her insight on the reasons men cheat, what makes someone a real man, what women like, what men like, and so much more. He shared a lot about himself, and she came to respect him as a man.

Amber and Josh eventually started dating, and because he was the first person she had dated since her breakup, she was cautious, though she was open and trusting. It was important for her to be able to determine if what Josh said aligned with what he did. She observed him and paid close attention to his actions, his statements, and his responses in situations.

Matthew 5:37 reveals the significance of honoring your word: If you say you are going to do something, then do it, and the same holds true if you say you are not going to do something, the expectation is that you will not do it. In your relationship, you should be able to rely on what your man or husband says. By opening his mouth, he is making a covenant with the Lord and is expected to fulfill what he said. Because no one is perfect, a man does and will fall short on occasion, but it will not be for lack of trying. The Coward, in comparison, does not live up to his word, simply because he has no intention of keeping his word; he says what he thinks you want to hear.

 **Pay Attention!** *Do not ignore the small, still voice telling you to move away from the relationship; that is God saving you from the trap of the devil. Stay focused and follow God's instruction. "My sheep listen to my voice," John 10:27 reminds us.*

One of the interesting things about Josh was that he regularly brought God into his conversations with Amber. He told her, "God is all over our relationship," and warned her, "Do not mess up your blessing" (remember the flip-trick?), though it was him messing things up. He told her that he would never cheat on her and that he would leave her if she were to cheat on him, but he cheated during their entire relationship. His days started and ended with him sending sexually based text messages to multiple women and requesting photos of them. He continued telling Amber how blessed he was to have her and how he anticipated a long and loving future with her, but all the while, his fear of being monogamous prevented their storybook ending. One day, Amber was on her way to take lunch to Josh when he told her not to come. She later learned that he had been out having lunch with one of his girlfriends.

Before they had become a serious couple, Josh would tell Amber that real men do not cheat or lie, that a real man takes care of his woman, that if a man does cheat on his woman, he is not serious about the relationship because when a man really cares for a woman and wants to be with her, he puts her first, even before himself. By his own admission, he was not a man.

Then, that little voice inside of her said, "Amber, this is not the one. He is just like [your ex]." She realized that Josh was not the man he claimed to be and had not put his childlike ways behind him. She detached from her feelings, however, and remained in the relationship out of convenience and to interrupt her boredom. Instead of being obedient and heeding the message of the Spirit, went along for the ride because a part of her hoped Josh would get it together.

He did not. Josh continued to enjoy his worldly life and served himself while Amber defied God because it felt better to have someone, even though he was the wrong one, than no one. This is another challenge women often encounter; we would rather be in a relationship just so we can have someone instead of patiently waiting for the right one. It is better to wait on the Lord and to be without while He prepares you for the union with your godly man. Faith that God is perfect is your conduit to fulfill God's glorious purpose for you.

Several months after Amber realized that Josh was not the man he claimed to be, their relationship abruptly ended after a volatile argument. Amber could no longer handle Josh's lies or his inability to live up to what he said, and Josh easily walked away because he was never fully invested in her or the relationship. She had come to the point of no longer having any respect for him, and her self-respect was waning. It is hard to return to a loving, even likable, relationship once respect has been lost in such a hurtful and cowardly way. Several months went by and Josh started calling Amber and enticing her to give him another chance. He wanted her to erase the bad moments and focus on the good, and prove that he was a changed man (though it would later be revealed that his desire to win her back was based solely on her fulfilling his sexual needs). She would not agree to move forward unless he agreed to go to counseling to see if a relationship was possible.

Shortly after agreeing to counseling, they attended their first session and Josh revealed a very interesting and important item: he had been unable to tell his mother that he and Amber were no longer together. He would have to admit his duplicitousness, a character trait he thought best to keep from his mother; he did not want his mother to know that he was not the man she had raised him to be. His cowardice would not allow him to accept the truth and deal with the discomfort or embarrassment that comes with that admission. Even when Amber brought up his deceit with her in a session, he asked her not to talk about it because, in his cowardice, he could not bear to hear his ugly truth.

Josh was an extreme case of cowardice. Most couples are able to discuss and openly admit their flaws and to own their roles with respect to relational challenges, but Josh was incapable of participating in that conversation with Amber or of acknowledging his role in their relationship's problems.

Josh lived his cowardice from the onset of his relationship with Amber. There are, however, individuals who experience a delayed display of cowardice. Olivia, for example, found her husband, Chad, experiencing delayed cowardice. Olivia and Chad came to see me for urgent marriage counseling because they had talked of divorce and she had already asked him to leave their home.

As Chad had courted Olivia, he appeared to be a good man. He had asked her to make the lifelong commitment of marriage, and she had excitedly agreed. About one year after their wedding, they were expecting their first baby, and reality caught up to Chad. He realized that marriage and family were "real" and that forever is a long time. It finally hit him that his days of bachelorhood and selfishness were gone and that he had to step up and be a man. There were nights he wanted to hang out with coworkers for happy hour and could not because family things needed to be done and his very pregnant wife needed support. There were nights he wanted to have friends over but household chores and preparing for a new baby were the priorities.

Chad saw that he was not ready to live the life he had thought he wanted, and his overwhelming fears kicked in: his fear of living a life with one woman, of relinquishing his player card, and of leaving his worldly life. He allowed his fear to decide that he was going to live the life he had lived before marriage and that his commitments to his wife and child would not continue to change him. He started making decisions without consulting his wife, going out after work with female colleagues, and not inviting his wife to work events where employees were encouraged to bring their significant others. He even accepted a new job that would require him to travel 50 percent of the time, and with a very attractive female coworker. Olivia and Chad had previously discussed not accepting any job that required travel for the first few years of raising their child.

Chad was afraid of living a life that he had confessed he desired to live. He had grown up in a very religious family, and finding a wife and settling down with kids had been regularly cited to him as the direction he should and would follow. Not only was Chad afraid of settling down and being a man, he was afraid to share with his family that he was not ready for that responsibility.

Unfortunately, being a coward led Chad to act on his attraction to his colleague, move out of his home while his wife was left to take care of a young baby, and break the covenant he had made with God and his wife. At first glance, it appeared that Chad was not afraid of commitment because he willingly walked to the altar of marriage with Olivia, but after fourteen months of marriage, the Coward was revealed. He could no longer live up to the promise he had made, in front of family and friends, to honor and love his wife.

Mark 4:17 may provide an explanation for Chad's cowardly actions: "But since they have no root, they last only a short time. When trouble or persecution comes because of the word, they quickly fall away." Cowards are not rooted in the Word of God and do not know God, but they are good at making people believe they are courageous; not until the perfect storm arrives is their cowardice exposed.

The Bible tells many stories of cowards not following God's instruction and instead taking matters into their own hands, concluding with them missing out on God's intended blessing. In Numbers 13, Moses sent twelve spies into Canaan, the Promised Land, to determine its landscape, inhabitants, resources, and occupancy. The twelve men were leaders of the twelve tribes of Israel. Ten of the twelve dismally reported that they would be unsuccessful in attempting to take over the land because the people living there were giants with strength surpassing their own. The remaining two, Joshua and Caleb, said it would be possible to take possession of the land and they were ready to do so. The ten who had concluded that it was impossible were, in essence, cowards who did not know the power or authority of God. Is it possible that these leaders had forgotten God's tremendous works, including delivering them from the Egyptians parting the Red Sea, providing food and water, guiding them day and night, and leading them to their new home? Was God's word not enough to convince all twelve leaders that they had everything they needed to take over the land promised to them by Him?

As a result of the other men's cowardice, Caleb and Joshua were the only two individuals from the original group of Israelites who followed Moses out of Egypt to enter Canaan. Those who had cowered under the possibility of fighting giants—including their leader, Moses—were denied entrance because they had refused when God had instructed the Israelites to take the land after leading them there.

When a Coward is faced with difficult decisions, it is not uncommon for him to reveal his true nature, as was the case with Chad and the disciple Peter. Peter (formerly known as Simon) was one of Jesus' most devout and dedicated followers. Jesus had handpicked Simon to become His disciple, simply stating, "Follow me" (Matthew 4:19), and Simon had dropped what he was doing to follow Jesus. But Jesus knew that fear was a part of Peter's composition.

During the time Jesus was on Earth teaching and performing miracles, Peter was by his side and became part of Jesus' inner circle. He was an enthusiastic student who celebrated His good works and did all he could to learn from the Master. Though not readily observable, his deeply rooted fear was always present and was exposed in situations when trust in the Lord was needed and expected. Matthew 14:28–31 documents one such scenario delivering a glimpse of Peter's fear: Peter saw Jesus walking on water and called, "'Lord, if it's you, tell me to come to you on the water." "Come," Jesus told him. Peter got out of the boat, walked on the water, and came toward Jesus, but when he saw the wind, he was afraid and, beginning to sink, cried, "Lord, save me!" Immediately, Jesus reached out his hand and caught Peter, saying, "You of little faith, why did you doubt?"

Though it appeared that Peter had enough courage to walk on water with Jesus, his confidence and boldness quickly waned as the winds began to blow violently. He retreated to his safe place, and the other disciples saw, perhaps for the first time, that Peter was not as brave as they had thought and that his fear was more powerful than his trust in the Lord.

Another example that sheds light on Peter's cowardice Peter is found in Matthew 16:21–23, in which Jesus told His disciples that He was going to suffer a great deal and be killed. Peter vehemently rebuked Him and told Him that it would never happen to Him. Jesus replied, "Get behind me, Satan! You are a stumbling block to me; you do not have in mind the concerns of God, but merely human concerns." His response highlights Peter's characteristics in common with the traits of satan, who is, by definition, a coward.

An additional example is shared in Luke 22:54–62, when Peter denied knowing Jesus—three times—on the night Jesus was arrested:

"Then seizing Him, they led Him away and took Him into the house of the high priest. Peter followed at a distance. And when some there had kindled a fire in the middle of the courtyard and had sat down together, Peter sat down with them. A servant girl saw him seated there in the firelight. She looked closely at him and said, "This man was with him." But he denied it. "Woman, I don't know him," he said. A little later someone else saw him and said, "You also are one of them." "Man, I am not!" Peter replied. About an hour later another asserted, "Certainly this fellow was with him, for he is a Galilean." Peter replied, "Man, I don't know what you're talking about!" Just as he was speaking, the rooster crowed. The Lord turned and looked straight at Peter. Then Peter remembered the word the Lord had spoken to him: "Before the rooster crows today, you will disown me three times." And he went outside and wept bitterly.

Earlier in the day, before Jesus was arrested, Jesus had told Peter that he would deny knowing Jesus three times. Peter had completely rejected this statement because, as a God-fearing follower of Jesus, he would never disavow Jesus.

From this passage, we learn that Peter followed Jesus from a distance in order to not be seen by the guards or to publicize his intimate relationship with Jesus; he did not want to make known his connection to the Lord. After the third time he denied knowing Jesus and the rooster crowed, Peter began to weep in his cowardice.

Even in the midst of Peter's cowardice, Jesus loved him and forgave him. After the Resurrection and His additional forty days on Earth, Jesus departed to sit at the right hand of God in heaven and Peter boldly preached the gospel without fear or worry of facing persecution. Just as Peter became a strong, courageous, and faith-filled man, so did Chad. After intense counseling that produced a heart change and a new perspective and understanding of God's love and grace, Chad returned home with a greater appreciation for his wife and their family, though months earlier, he had been willing to walk away from them for the sake of short-term gratification. This is proof that God changes things. If you believe you are in a relationship with a coward, there is hope if he is willing to work and to turn to the Lord for help and strength. His actions will show if he is willing to trust in the Lord.

God has given you the ability to utilize your heart (where He resides) and your mind (the knowledge He allows you to have) to make godly decisions in your life. It is important to keep in mind that a man who loves Jesus also has the same loving abilities to use his heart and mind and should recognize the Jesus (His

Spirit) in you and treat you accordingly. You are also charged to recognize the Jesus in your significant other and to love, respect, cherish, and support your man. Your heart and mind, along with his, should work in tandem as you both compassionately acknowledge the Spirit in each other.

The letter of James 1:21–25 boldly declares the following:

> Therefore, get rid of all moral filth and the evil that is so prevalent and humbly accept the word planted in you, which can save you. Do not merely listen to the word, and so deceive yourselves. Do what it says. Anyone who listens to the word but does not do what it says is like someone who looks at his face in a mirror and, after looking at himself, goes away and immediately forgets what he looks like. But whoever looks intently into the perfect law that gives freedom, and continues in it—not forgetting what they have heard, but doing it— they will be blessed in what they do.

In present-day relationship terms, this passage means that a coward deceives himself and others, and though he may portray himself as living according to the Word, he is far removed from it. A man of God, in contrast, makes the effort to follow the Word and to treat people accordingly. He knows that he is supposed to care for others first and to walk a selfless path. He esteems the contract he makes when he gives his word, and he is blessed because of his obedience.

As you take a moment to reflect, you may recognize some traits of your man that indicate he is a Coward. For example:

- He might say a lot to prove his commitment to you, but when it comes time to act upon that commitment, he doesn't.

- He may talk about God in the relationship, but his actions show that a worldly relationship, rather than a godly one, is his priority.

- He is afraid to do what is right and to honor his promises, his oath to you, and his covenant to the Lord.

God's perfect love for you wants the absolute best for you, and He is saddened to see you hurting, being mistreated, or relying on the world to guide your decisions. The good news is that you can make a decision to trust God and have faith in what He says, and if your man is willing, God can help him do so as well.

If you find that your relationship is the antithesis of a healthy and loving relationship, the necessary first step is to identify the cause of the relationship's problems and take a look at yourself. Be mindful of the fact that one of God's greatest commandments is to love others like you love yourself. If you find that you are not loving yourself as God intended but that you accept and accommodate your man's unloving or ungodly actions, it is time to power up and make some changes.

On the first day of 2016, I reached out to a man I have known since I was six years old, to wish him a happy and blessing-filled new year. Our parents were great friends, and I used to babysit him and his younger siblings. I was unable to reach him, so I left him a voice mail sharing my well wishes for him and his family. When he returned my call I, unfortunately, was unavailable, and he left me a message in kind. In his message, he shared that he and his lady had gone away for the holiday and were just returning from a wonderful vacation. I thought, *This is a man. He is excited about sharing the good news of his relationship. He is not trying to keep it a secret. He will shout from the rooftops "I have a lady and we do fun things together! Though you did not ask, I want to share and be open about my relationship because she is my lady and everyone should know that I have her!"*

You will find that men do this—they are excited to talk about the woman in their lives! Listening to men speak of their women is like listening to someone whose favorite sports team just won the championship, not like someone who had to sit and watch his least favorite chick flick.

In contrast, it is normal to find that the Coward will not offer that he is in a relationship. Most boys, even when asked, will downplay their relationship, if they mention it at all. Former client Keith did this. He gladly shared news about his new business, but not about the baby he and Nancy had on the way. He kept his circle updated about him traveling with his pastor, but not that he was engaged. He freely talked about the joy of coaching basketball but kept his girlfriend a secret. These were all red flags that Nancy turned a blind eye to but that the Spirit was alerting her to. It was her desire to listen to the world and to ignore the still, small voice because she desperately wanted to believe that Keith would change and become the man he promised he was.

A man, not a Coward, is a person of faith and deeds. God makes clear that a person's actions must coincide with his or her words. If a man speaks faith and fidelity, his actions will demonstrate the same. If he speaks love, honor, and commitment, his actions will demonstrate them. A man will bear the fruits of the spirit, which are love, joy, peace, patience, kindness, goodness, faithfulness, gentleness, and self-control, and each will be evident in his actions. He will put you first and deny selfish ambition. He will not lose his temper or cause you harm commonly in your relationship. He will understand with certainty that you are a gift from God, and because he sees the Jesus in you, he will joyfully embrace who you are with patience and gentleness:

> What good is it, my brothers and sisters, if someone claims to have faith but has no deeds? Can such faith save them? Suppose a brother or a sister is without clothes and daily food. If one of you says to them, "Go in peace; keep warm and well fed," but does nothing about their physical needs, what good is it? In the same way, faith by itself, if it is not accompanied by action, is dead. But someone will say, "You have faith; I have deeds." Show me your faith without deeds, and I will show you my faith by my deeds. You believe that there is one God. Good! Even the demons believe that—and shudder. You foolish person, do you want evidence that faith without deeds is useless? Was not our father Abraham considered righteous for what he did when he offered his son Isaac on the altar? You see that his faith and his actions were working together, *and his faith was made complete by what he did.* And the Scripture was fulfilled that says, "Abraham believed God, and it was credited to him as righteousness," and he was called God's friend. You see that a person is considered righteous *by what they do* and not by faith alone." (James 2:14–24; my emphasis)

It is not enough for your boy to say, "I love you," if what he does is contrary to God's definition of love. Again, God is not calling him to be perfect, but to regularly utilize his heart and mind to produce loving actions. God wants you to experience a godly love in your relationship, and if you are obedient and follow Him, rather than the world, you will.

## Helpful Scriptures

"The wicked flee though no one pursues, but the righteous are as bold as a lion." (Proverbs 28:1)

"Evildoers do not understand what is right, but those who seek the Lord understand it fully." (Proverbs 28:5)

## Activity

It is time to start trusting God in your relationship and to identify what He wants for you and make serious efforts to receive it. Make a preliminary list of what you believe God wants for you in your relationship. A month later, after you have spent time in His Word, make the list again and see if it is the same. As you continue to grow and develop a more intimate relationship with God, make another list at the three-month point and compare to the original list.

Today                    30 days from now            90 days from now

_____          _____          _____

_____          _____          _____

_____          _____          _____

_____          _____          _____

_____          _____          _____

_____          _____          _____

_____          _____          _____

_____          _____          _____

Compare your three lists. What changes were made, and what stayed the same? How have these changes affected you and your relationship, if at all?

_____

_____

_____

_____

_____

What do you think are the main reasons you are or are not seeing change?

_____

_____

_____

_____

_____

It is important to recognize your strength in a relationship and to ensure that your wants and desires are recognized and fulfilled. Do you feel that both you and your significant other celebrate your relationship in truth and faith? If not, what changes can you make and what discussions can you have that will promote each person to have the courage to trust God and thereby be honest with each other?

_____

_____

_____

_____

_____

## Prayer

Father, I come to You today giving thanks for all You are. You are my provider, my comforter, my guide, and my healer. I have been hurt by cowardly men who are too afraid to seek and honor You. They run from godly relationships and treat me as a woman in the world, and I am ready for a change! The love You have for me and want me to experience is what I want moving forward. I have not always listened to Your still, small voice, and I ask for forgiveness. I am ready to be obedient and to do what You have called me to do, but I cannot do it without You. You are my saving grace and my source of strength. I pray that as I grow in You, You will help me discern who is of You and who is not. It is Your love that I want to receive and give, and I am thankful that You have already identified the man for me. Thank You, Father. In Jesus' name I pray. Amen.

# 4

# THE USER

*Get wisdom, get understanding; do not forget my words or turn away from them.*

—Proverbs 4:5

*T*he User is the fourth and final type of boy discussed in this volume. Though he shares similar traits with his counterparts, the User has definitive differences setting him apart. He does not use women only for sex; more planning and thinking than that is involved when the User plans/plots. In yesteryear, it was common for men to use women for sex and then tell their friends all about it. It was called locker room talk. Some had to work really hard, but others, not as much. Regardless, what was most important to the User was that he set out to conquer and he was successful. Today, things are different because there are additional motivations.

Now, women exercise their rights to have more and, as such, have acquired a significant trove, meaning they have more to offer and more for Users to take. We can now be owners of houses and luxury cars, with money in the bank and professional careers that afford us niceties. A woman can even get pregnant without a man being physically present. The User will seek to benefit from such women and their many accomplishments.

The Bible contains several stories of users, people who take advantage of others for the sole purpose of self-advancement. One story that stands out is in Genesis 12:10–20. Abram, the man God promised would be the father of many nations, used his wife, Sarai, to save his life. A grave famine took place in their land, so Abram and Sarai traveled to Egypt to escape the dire circumstances. Before they entered Egypt, Abram told Sarai, "I know what a beautiful woman you are. When the Egyptians see you, they will say, 'This is his wife.' Then they will kill me but will let you live. Say you are my sister, so that I will be treated well for your sake and my life will be spared because of you" (Genesis 12:11–13). Abram persuaded his wife to denounce their marriage and then to become part of the king's harem so Abram would be treated well by the king.

When they entered Egypt, all Abram said came to pass: "When Abram came to Egypt, the Egyptians saw that Sarai was a very beautiful woman. And when Pharaoh's officials saw her, they praised her to Pharaoh, and she was taken into his palace. He treated Abram well for her sake, and Abram acquired sheep and cattle, male and female donkeys, male and female servants, and camels" (Genesis 12:14–16). Though Abram was willing to allow the king to have his way with Sarai, God was not. God caused the king to be stricken with disease so he would not be able to touch Sarai. Then the king realized that he was the recipient of the disease because Sarai was Abram's wife rather than his sister: "But the Lord inflicted serious diseases on Pharaoh and his household because of Abram's wife Sarai. So Pharaoh summoned Abram. 'What have you done to me?' he said. 'Why didn't you tell me she was your wife? Why did you say, 'She is my sister,' so that I took her to be my wife? Now then, here is your wife. Take her and go!' Then Pharaoh gave orders about Abram to his men, and they sent him on his way, with his wife and everything he had" (Genesis 12: 17–20).

Though God and Abram had had a trusting relationship, Abram failed to trust God during this time and looked out for his own interests. His thoughts had not been on God providing a method of escape or protecting Sarai; rather, Abram had been consumed with selfish ambition to ensure he was taken care of while another man had his wife.

Remember that I said in Chapter 3 that Keith, Nancy's former fiancé, was a multiple boy-card carrier? Add the User card to the list. Nancy shows love by helping others, but she did not know about setting boundaries. Sadly, Keith took for granted the love and kindness she displayed, and Nancy realized too late that she should have placed boundaries around her giving in the beginning of their relationship.

The majority of women do not mind taking care of their men. It is instinctual to nurture, and most women are joyously obliged to do so; however, boundaries must be put in place in the early phases of your relationship. Women should not provide everything for their men, for a couple of reasons. First, he will have nothing to look forward to if you plateau and give all you have (physically, emotionally, mentally) in the first few months. Second, your generous giving will likely set his expectations and could become the sole reason for him to stay with you.

In a sermon not too long ago, my pastor, Bishop Walter S. Thomas, Sr., discussed the topic of using people, saying, "Folk will cut you loose in a heartbeat. People have relationships for promotion. In other words, I will hook myself to you as long as you can take me somewhere. It is a relationship that is totally predicated on utilitarianism. I relate to you, but the reality of it is I use you to get what I want. Not to become who I am meant to be. In order to become, I can't use, but to get, I can use you." The validity and accuracy of this statement shines light on the demise of the Spirit in our lives while offering insight into why we must battle to receive godly men. Can you recall being in a relationship in which you felt your man was the only one benefitting?

One of the main purposes of having people in your life is to grow collectively. God places people in our lives for reasons, but those reasons never include to use or to be used, only to edify. When you truly have the love of Jesus in your heart, you desire to see the people around you experience lives full of joy and abundant overflow. Moving your focus from yourself to others opens the gates for the Lord to abundantly bless you.

A man using you for his own self-promotion is adversarial, at best. Throughout the Bible, we can see the devil using people to accomplish his plan of destruction and to interrupt God's plan for those people's lives:

- Satan used Eve to go against God by encouraging her to eat the fruit from the forbidden tree. He deceived her by declaring God a liar and encouraged her to disobey God's commands so she could become like God. (Genesis 3)

- Lot and his wife were warned not to turn around as their home city of Sodom was destroyed. I can picture satan whispering in the ear of Lot's wife: "Turn around and have one more look. Nothing will happen to you." She turned into a pillar of salt, used to destroy her relationship with Lot and to go against a directive from God. (Genesis 19)

- The Lord told Solomon not to intermarry with women of other nations. He married 700 princesses and had 300 concubines from various nations, and, as a result, he turned away from God and began worshipping idols and false gods. (1 Kings 11)

- The lust that David experienced while watching Bathsheba bathe caused him to commit acts that the Lord detests: adultery and murder. (2 Samuel 11)

- Sarah did not trust that the Lord would give her and Abraham a child, so she used Hagar, her maidservant, to conceive with Abraham. Hagar gave birth to Ishmael. After Sarah gave birth to Isaac 13 years later, she became frustrated with Ishmael and Hagar, and she told Abraham to banish them both. The result was the creation of two nations. (Genesis 16)

- Judas accepted money from the chief priests to turn Jesus over. He later hanged himself as a result of his betrayal. The adversary was quite pleased with what he had accomplished using Judas. (Matthew 26)

Let's return to Amber and Josh. Like Keith, Josh carried multiple boy cards—in this case, the Coward card. Amber and Josh are a good example of how failing to implement necessary boundaries can lead to the exploitation of kindness. Josh started dating Amber at the start of a difficult time for him. He had lost all of his money when the market crashed and was experiencing a profound financial struggle. He could not pay his bills, rent, or child support, or even buy groceries. Amber was able to support him for a few months, but she let him know that he would have to start helping her out financially after he got through his arduous period. They agreed that he would take over her mortgage and other bills when he was back on his feet. She spent more than $50,000 in six months with him, paying his rent, cable, utility, and phone bills; paying his bail after he was arrested for not paying child support; buying his groceries; giving him spending money and gas money; taking him out to eat; and paying for his car repairs.

Keep in mind, the agreement was that Josh would take over Amber's house payments. The moment he was back on his feet, however, they had an argument and he left. He benefitted from her kindness, and once he had gotten everything he needed, he left her in a financial quandary. It has been many years since their relationship ended, and he has never offered to fulfill their agreement and return the money he promised to repay, which hurt Amber financially and emotionally. Recall that Josh and Amber had known each other for years before they dated, and from what she knew of him, he was a stand-up guy. During the time he was going through this hardship, however, Josh cheated on Amber and lied to her. There was nothing godly or manly about this boy who claimed to be a man of God. Remember, a man thinks of others and practices selfless acts.

After Josh was back on his feet, he did not check in with Amber to see how she was doing or if he could help her out in any way. In a recent conversation with me, Amber mentioned that she hears from Josh regularly to meet for "late-night hookups" and he continues to assert that he loves her. This causes her to feel frustrated and confused and makes her briefly question if she made the wrong decision to end the relationship. Unfortunately, it appears that Josh is a forty-something boy who has been unable to trust God and remove the hold that the adversary has over him. He allows the world to guide him and his decision-making and keeps God at a distance in his relationships and his life. Though this seems like an extreme scenario, it happens all too frequently with children of God.

> **Pay Attention!** *Satan will make you question what your spirit is telling you.*

When Amber started her sessions with me, she was hoping to understand what had happened with Josh and why, and to heal her broken heart. Upon completion of our sessions, she felt empowered and ready to move forward in a healthy relationship, understood the need for boundaries in relationships, and also understood balance and what a healthy relationship looks like. She was able to forgive Josh and was grateful that God had removed him from her life. Though the experience cost her almost $55,000, she realized it could have cost her more than that. She also learned that when God closes a door, it is best to not reopen it. Those regular text messages and phone calls from Josh were the adversary doing what he does best—tempting her to go against God's will for her life. Amber was certain that God did not want her with Josh, but satan will make you question what your spirit is telling you.

Relationships are serious business; they are not to be taken lightly. You take a relationship lightly by making decisions based on selfish motivations and not on the Father. If you find that you are in a relationship with a User, it is important that you understand why. Quite often, when someone stays in a relationship that is one-sided, it is because of personal insecurities or low self-esteem. It could also be because of a desire to be needed or to take care of someone. It is important to get to the root of the issue that causes you to believe you should stay in a relationship contrary to what the Father wants for you. Do you lack faith? Are you not confident of who you are in Christ and of what He wants for you?

I spoke to a thirty-five-year-old single man recently, and he shared that he had advised a female friend who has been unsuccessful in dating good men. Her last relationship had ended in a breakup that had left her hurting, and the men she had dated since had sex with her and then ended their communication. He explained to his friend that men are like animals that can detect wounded prey. Because they can sense her vulnerable state, they take advantage of it. But the same guys who took advantage of the vulnerability can also sense a strong woman who knows what she wants and will treat her with respect. He told her that she has to get over her bruised emotions and return to being a strong and confident woman. The User knows how to use your experiences, emotions, and feelings for his benefit because he allows society, not God, to dictate how he treats women; he sees someone or something he wants and plays the game to win what he wants; and he wants bragging rights so he can show the world that he was able to "win."

Here are some clues to help you identify if your significant other carries the User card:

- He does not regularly demonstrate his love.

- He continues to ask for your help and does not offer support to you.

- He makes everything about him and rarely about you.

- He is reluctant to give when you are in need.

- He does not do anything without you asking and never considers giving to you to be a blessing.

- His attitude or demeanor changes negatively if you deny one of his requests.

- He exhibits envy or jealousy toward you.

- He exudes selfish ambition.

When you look at your relationship, do you feel that the two of you make each other better and are growing together? Be wise. Be cognizant and aware of what is transpiring in your relationship. The Lord wants the best for you, and if you let Him guide you, you will receive the best! If you are experiencing low self-esteem or low self-worth, or if you feel the need to take care of someone, it is time to renew your mind and let the love and power of Jesus abound in your life. If you are in a relationship with a User—or any other boy type—it is time to reevaluate the relationship and make a decision about the next steps. As you do, think about God's best and what He wants for you in your relationship.

## Helpful Scriptures

"Pay attention and turn your ear to the sayings of the wise; apply your heart to what I teach, for it is pleasing when you keep them in your heart and have all of them ready on your lips." (Proverbs 22: 17–18)

"In their hearts humans plan their course, but the LORD establishes their steps." (Proverbs 16:9)

"The way of fools seems right to them, but the wise listen to advice." (Proverbs 12:15)

"I urge you, brothers and sisters, to watch out for those who cause divisions and put obstacles in your way that are contrary to the teaching you have learned. Keep away from them. For such people are not serving our Lord Christ, but their own appetites. By smooth talk and flattery they deceive the minds of naive people. Everyone has heard about your obedience, so I rejoice because of you; but I want you to be wise about what is good, and innocent about what is evil." (Romans 16:17–19)

"I can do all things through Him who gives me strength." (Philippians 4:13)

"Do not be yoked together with unbelievers. For what do righteousness and wickedness have in common? Or what fellowship can light have with darkness?" (2 Corinthians 6:14)

"Do not take advantage of each other, but fear your God. I am the LORD your God." (Leviticus 25:17)

"For even when we were with you, we gave you this rule: 'The one who is unwilling to work shall not eat.'" (2 Thessalonians 3:10)

## Activity

If you realize you are in a relationship with a User, what do you think are the main reasons you are staying in the relationship with him?

_____

_____

_____

_____

_____

Some of the Scriptures above highlight that God wants you to be wise, rely on Him, and not take advantage of each other. If you are being taken advantage of, it is a clear indication that the User is not actively making an effort to be the man

God has called him to be. God is letting you know that to stay clear of the User, you have to know His Word and keep it in your heart; seek wise counsel and not rely on encouragement from foolish people; and be wary of people who act in ways contrary to what the Lord says. God longs to have an intimate relationship with you. He wants you to turn to Him for everything, even your relationship, because He is your source for everything. He has an amazing man just for you, but to receive that man, you must do your part and be obedient to what He is telling you.

Knowing that God denounces people who take advantage of others, it is important that you identify ways you can eliminate being used. For example, you may want to create boundaries at the start of your relationship. If you are currently in a relationship with a User, you may want to have a discussion with him about what you are seeing and how that makes you feel. Discuss the possibility of becoming a team that supports and helps each other. Share with him your feelings and thoughts about ways he can be a blessing to you and what giving looks like. Then determine if the two of you are willing to be better together.

If something is holding your boy back from being the man he has been called to be, maybe the Lord is telling you to help him. If your boy is willing and able to make a God change by becoming the man God has called him to be, then try it and see. If you realize he has no intention of embracing the Spirit in your relationship, it is probably time to step away.

Meditate on Scripture and listen to what the Lord tells you and wants for you.

## Prayer

Lord, Your love, mercy, and grace are amazing. You give much to me all of the time, and I am forever grateful that though I may not always give of myself to You, You still bless me and give me what I need, and sometimes what I want! Lord, if I am going to be used, I pray to be used by You. I no longer want to be the vessel for selfish promotion but pray to be part of a two-sided relationship in which we honor You by honoring and helping to elevate each other. Today, I ask for Your guidance as I make the decision to be more cognizant of my relationship and to close the door to being used. I thank You for opening my eyes to the traits of the User. Lord, I need Your wisdom because I realize that I may not have utilized the best decision making when deciding to enter or stay in relationships. I confess that my reasons for entering or staying in relationships were not of you but were perhaps from a desire to feel needed or to take care of others, but I must have healthy boundaries in place for my giving. Though I do not give to receive, I remember that it is important to be appreciated and not be taken advantage of. I am extremely grateful that You will return tenfold everything that has been taken from me. I do understand that this does not just include tangible items but also my heart and spirit. I pray for Your loving spirit to surround the User in my relationship, and let Your will be done. I love You and pray these things in Jesus' name. Amen.

# II: A REAL MAN: WHAT GOD WANTS YOU TO KNOW ABOUT REAL MEN

*Then we will no longer be infants, tossed back and forth by the waves, and blown here and there by every wind of teaching and by the cunning and craftiness of people in their deceitful scheming. Instead, speaking the truth in love, we will grow to become in every respect the mature body of him who is the head, that is, Christ. From him the whole body, joined and held together by every supporting ligament, grows and builds itself up in love, as each part does its work.*

—Ephesians 4:14–16

*G*od wants you, as a child of the Most High, to be wise, informed, and equipped to effectively handle relationships and the challenges that arise within them. He also wants you to recognize what a man is and what to expect in your relationship with a man. God has certain expectations of your man, and so should you! He created man to be loving, kind, compassionate, honest, and respectful, and to have faith. It is important to God that you are able to determine who is of Him and who is not. It is equally important that you are able to enjoy a healthy relationship with healthy disagreements and challenges as you lovingly and respectfully work through them with God's help. This section will reveal in more detail what a man looks and acts like, according to God's definition.

# 5

# WHAT IS A MAN?

*When I was a child, I talked like a child, I thought like a child,*
*I reasoned like a child. When I became a man, I put the ways of*
*childhood behind me.*

—1 Corinthians 13:11

*W*e grow up believing that the criteria for becoming a man are reaching a certain age, having a job, graduating from college, and renting or owning a home. We have been led to believe that manhood naturally occurs at one or more of these benchmarks, but the Word of God reveals differently. God reveals that manhood begins when a boy puts the ways of childhood to rest and becomes complete in the love of Jesus.

Putting the ways of childhood to rest means relinquishing the behaviors of and belief in the world and making a conscious decision to put others first because of the love of Jesus that dwells within. For example, someone who has put to rest the ways of childhood willing renounces any dishonest or self-absorbed behavior and embraces the attributes of love. When a boy transitions to a man, he understands his role as a man of God and makes an effort to live that role. When a boy becomes a man, he abandons the thoughts, speech, and reasoning of a child, which are normally centered on getting what he wants. Not all attributes that children have will be poor traits in manhood (for example, innocence, love, kindness, and compassion), but those traits that accompany the ways of the world and are particularly self-centered can be detrimental to a man. Though a real man will fall short, which is expected, he does try to follow the Spirit and not the world. He will put away the games that he played in "childhood," which may have included being unfaithful, using women, abusing women, and pretending to be something he was not. A man understands that he does not need to engage in behavior that is contrary to what God has called him to be. He has a genuinely authentic desire to pursue Jesus and to love and edify you and others.

Becoming complete in the love of Jesus means unleashing the spirit and love of God into every area of one's life. This is not proven by someone's words but by observable actions. An indication of true promotion or advancement into manhood is marked by a man with God's Spirit who trusts in Him, has faith, and is obedient. His works make clear that he is a real man. You can see it in the way he communicates with people and observe it in the way he treats you and others. He demonstrates a consistent effort to love and to help others with a positive attitude.

When a comparison is made between God's definition and the world's definition of man, you will find they are distinctly different:

## The World's Definition

(per Merriam-Webster's online dictionary)

- An adult male human being

- A man or boy who shows the qualities (such as strength and courage) that men are traditionally supposed to have

- A woman's husband or boyfriend

God's Definition

- The crown of God's creation (Genesis 1:28-30)

- Made in God's image, in His likeness (Genesis 1:26-27)

Merriam-Webster's definition confirms the criteria for defining manhood that we learn and believe as we grow, mature, and start dating; this definition indicates that when a male reaches the age of eighteen, has manly qualities like physical strength or has a significant other, he is a man. God's definition refutes what the world says, however, and boldly and emphatically declares that a man is made in the image of God and is the crown of God's glory. But what does this mean?

The image of God includes several components: human body, ability to reason, distinctiveness, authority to rule, morality, and ability to love. These necessary components are the means for him to attain the status of man under the authority that God has given him. Genesis 1:26-30 confirms that men have these components. The Joseph Benson Commentary on the Old and New Testaments provides this accurate summation: "As such, man's body is erect and endowed with speech that he may give the word of command. In God's image is man's soul, his spirit. Man's spirit, like God's spirit, is immaterial, invisible, active, intelligent, free and immortal. And when man is first created, he is endowed with a high degree of divine knowledge, and with holiness and righteousness." (http://biblehub.com/commentaries/genesis/1-26.htm)

Let us explore each component of a godly man, beginning with the human body: "God created man in His own image, in the image of God He created him; male and female He created them" (Genesis 1:27). God created the human body for man, for Adam and Eve. God Himself took on human form, as Jesus, to save us all from condemnation. God made man a ruler and made him distinct from all other created creatures. Though God is the sovereign ruler of the universe, man was created to rule over the animals and over certain parts of creation with his ability to reason, communicate, and make moral decisions. God also gave power to man, but power in the sense of humility. Man's beginnings from the dust of the earth—"The Lord God formed the man from the soil of the ground and breathed into his nostrils the breath of life, and the man became a living being" (Genesis 2:7)—speaks to the power of God that is in man, but also to his humble creation. Jesus, the most powerful man ever, was born in a barn with animals, flies, and feces. There was nothing regal or stately about His beginnings or the thirty-three years He spent on Earth, but His power was found in humility and humbleness and in the selfless acts he performed for everyone else.

Two of the most important traits of a godly man include his ability to love and his morality. God created man to love, because God is love: "Dear friends, let us love one another, for love comes from God. Everyone who loves has been born of God and knows God. Whoever does not love does not know God, because God is love" (1 John 4:7–8). The Spirit of God is love, and when a man has this Spirit, it is evident in everything he does. This is one reason that I repeatedly stress the importance of you receiving love from your man; it is one of the most important traits of manhood and is crucial for relational success.

Last, and certainly not least, is morality. God created man in His own image to be truthful and honest: "No one who practices deceit will dwell in My house; no one who speaks falsely will stand in My presence" (Psalm 101:7). Morality, a key component in determining a man's veracity, refers more to God's likeness than to His image. Morality shows an intimacy with God; it sheds light on someone's desire to be a real man. The possession of moral power is key in separating boys from men according to the biblical definition. Though I am not suggesting in any way that your man will or should be perfect because Jesus is perfect, I am sharing what God states are the traits of a man and that men should, with all their hearts, strive to be what God has called them to be in relationships and in all other ways. Though humans' image and likeness to God were tainted and weakened by the fall, both still exist; because of Jesus, both are expected of men.

Acts 6 introduces the seven men chosen by the Apostles to help support the administrative tasks of the ministry. Stephen was one of the seven selected because he was a man filled with faith and the Holy Spirit (see Acts 6:5). Stephen was an incredible example of one who possessed the godly traits of a man, and because he lived in God's image, he was persecuted: "Now Stephen, a man full of God's grace and power, performed great wonders and signs among the people. Opposition arose, however, from members of the Synagogue of the Freedmen (as it was called)—Jews of Cyrene and Alexandria as well as the provinces of Cilicia and Asia—who began to argue with Stephen. But they could not stand up against the wisdom the Spirit gave him as he spoke" (Acts 6:8–10). Because the men who argued with Stephen could not win their debate with him, they found and bribed men to falsely accuse Stephen of rebelling against the teachings of Moses and God. When they brought Stephen to face the Sanhedrin (the Jewish council of the court system), they provided these false witnesses to testify and to wrongly accuse Stephen of blasphemy.

When the high priest of the Sanhedrin asked Stephen if what was being said was true, Simon could have cowered, but instead, he passionately cited the truth of God, Abraham, Joseph, and Moses. Afterward, he continued to stand strong in his faith and in truth when he accused the Sanhedrin of unlawful conduct: being stiff-necked (in bigotry and pride), having uncircumcised hearts, resisting the Holy Spirit, killing the Messiah, and not obeying God's law. The court was wholly appalled and offended by his accusations, and it called for him to be stoned. Stephen, being a man of God, got the attention of Jesus, who stood at the right hand of God for him: "But Stephen, full of the Holy Spirit, looked up to heaven and saw the glory of God, and Jesus standing at the right hand of God. 'Look,' he said, 'I see heaven open and the Son of Man standing at the right hand of God'" (Acts 7:55–56).

I use this powerful example to show that in the face of death, Stephen was a man who boldly lived in truth and faith. Today, it is important that your man not succumb to the pressures of the world but stays rooted in the Word of God and stands on faith when facing difficult situations, relationally and otherwise.

Let us consider the morality principle as an essential litmus test in determining what card your man, or potential man, carries. It is easiest to do what feels good in the moment, and leaving the moral compass at the door is regularly the preferred choice of a boy when making decisions in a relationship. In contrast, a man will regularly and consistently do what is right because it honors you and God.

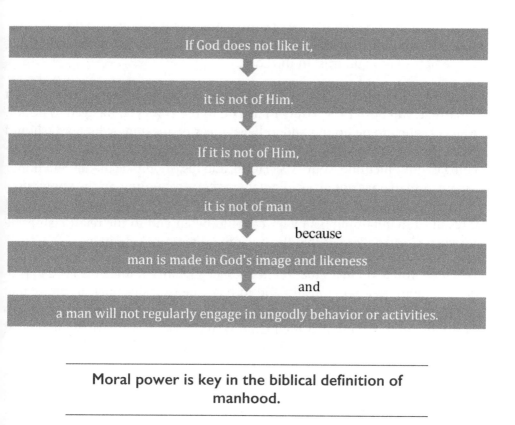

If God does not like it,

it is not of Him.

If it is not of Him,

it is not of man

because

man is made in God's image and likeness

and

a man will not regularly engage in ungodly behavior or activities.

---

**Moral power is key in the biblical definition of manhood.**

---

Earlier in the book, I referenced Nancy and Keith. Keith regularly fell into the trap of the adversary, neglecting morality to do what felt good in the moment. Despite having a pregnant girlfriend at home, Keith would not stop engaging in adulterous activity. After the two cried with each other, Keith promising to never do it again, and committing to couple's counseling, Nancy and Keith moved forward in their relationship together, knowing that the Lord could heal her broken heart and his wayward traits. A month later, they were engaged, and they continued to go through the tears and promises because he continued to cheat and lie after asking her to marry him.

Keith is just one example of how a boy is different from a man. Men are expected to be honest when they fail to live up to godly standards. A man makes morally sound decisions, and when he falls short, he tells the truth because he is made in the image and likeness of God. As a man, he can handle whatever comes his way as a result of his actions. A man has God's power, authority, and faith, and he uses and relies on them. You see, a man understands that God rewards obedience, and he understands that even when he messes up, God wants him to be honest and to be a representative of Christ. A boy will continue to lie and cover up his mistakes until the very end, but a man will rise up and do the right thing because of his faith and trust in the Lord.

A man of faith is called to live up to his word, to the promises he makes. If you are married, you both have a duty to live up to the vows you pledged to honor. We are all called to be honest and to have integrity, meaning your "yes" should mean yes and your "no" should be no (Matthew 5:37). Simply put, if he says he is going to do something, your expectation, and his, should be that he will honor his word. A man does not make idle statements or commitments; he knows how important keeping his word is and has every intention of living up to it. Even if the result of maintaining his integrity could be an end to the relationship, he fully trusts God and knows that the outcome is part of God's plan.

So what are you to do in a situation like Nancy's? Nancy wanted the Lord to provide healing in their relationship and to have the cohesive nuclear family that Keith promised. She wanted that for their child, and she was going to do whatever it took to make sure that their child would have it—but she ignored what God was telling her to do. Her spirit told her to end her relationship with Keith, but Keith kept insisting that they would be together.

Remember, God will let you know what to do, but it is up to you to listen and to heed what He tells you. Matthew 6:33 tells us: "But seek first His kingdom and His righteousness, and all these things will be given to you as well." God is very clear about us seeking Him first—then He will provide everything: our clothing, food, finances…and mates too. When God is involved in your life, including your relationships, you can trust that you are with the person He intends if you follow His voice: "My sheep listen to my voice; I know them, and they follow Me" (John 10:27). I see regularly in clients (and celebrity couples) who wed and wed again and again that they are seeking not the Father, but self-satisfaction. When we do not seek Him in everything, what we intend will not flourish.

---

**God only wants the best for you and that includes a healthy, happy, and loving relationship.**

---

Even when we do not listen to Him, God has a plan that gets us to the place He has been nudging us to go all along. God saw that Keith's chronic and unsafe infidelity were not enough for Nancy to leave him alone, so God had to do something that would be the mother of all wake-up calls. One night, Keith grabbed her arm and began twisting it, punched her in the chest, and pushed her face-first into a wall. That was all Nancy needed to finally obey the guidance she had rejected for so long. There was no questioning or doubting what she had to do. She was not going to stick around to be hit again; she did not need anything else to open her eyes so she could see Keith for who he really was: a boy. Unfortunately, because she had not listened to God's gentle voice when He had told her to walk away during the early phases of her relationship, God had to do something drastic and dramatic that caused her a lot of physical and emotional hurt and pain.

In our counseling sessions, Nancy often focused on the past, saying, "If only I had listened months ago…" We cannot dwell on the past and what could have, would have, or should have been, however. What we can, however, do is focus on making the right decisions now and getting powered up! I do hope that through sharing Nancy's story, it confirms for you the importance of listening to God's voice and saving yourself and your family from experiencing your own tragic wake-up call.

## Helpful Scriptures

"Therefore, my beloved brethren, be steadfast, immovable, always abounding in the work of the Lord, knowing that your toil is not in vain in the Lord." (1 Corinthians 15:58)

"You younger men, likewise, be subject to your elders; and all of you, clothe yourselves with humility toward one another, for God is opposed to the proud, but gives grace to the humble. Therefore humble yourselves under the mighty hand of God, that He may exalt you at the proper time, casting all your anxiety on Him, because He cares for you." (1 Peter 5:5–7)

"For even the Son of Man did not come to be served, but to serve, and to give His life a ransom for many." (Mark 10:45)

"To this you were called, because Christ suffered for you, leaving you an example, that you should follow in his steps." (1 Peter 2:21)

## Activity

Describe your definition of a man.

_____

_____

_____

_____

_____

Describe God's definition of a man.

_____

_____

_____

_____

_____

Is your definition the same as God's definition?

_____

_____

_____

_____

_____

If there are differences between the definitions, what role do you think this has played or is playing in your relationships?

_____

_____

_____

_____

_____

If you start using God's definition of man, how will this change your outlook on future relationships?

_____

_____

_____

_____

_____

## Prayer

Father, I come to You with an open heart to receive Your wisdom. Lord, shower me with Your knowledge and wisdom, and allow it to lead me in my relationship and everything I do. Today may have been the first time I truly had a glimpse into what a real man is and what Your expectation of man is, both in and out of relationships. Thank You for sharing this eye-opening and life-changing revelation with me, and thank You for caring enough about me to want the absolute best for me and my man. I know that the man You have destined for me is a real man and will honor You in everything. I love You, Lord. In Jesus' name I pray. Amen.

# 6.

# THE ROLE OF A MAN

*Blessed (happy, fortunate, prosperous, and enviable) is the man who walks and lives not in the counsel of the ungodly [following their advice, their plans and purposes], nor stands [submissive and inactive] in the path where sinners walk, nor sits down [to relax and rest] where the scornful [and the mockers] gather. But his delight and desire are in the law of the Lord, and on His law (the precepts, the instructions, the teachings of God) he habitually meditates (ponders and studies) by day and by night. And he shall be like a tree firmly planted [and tended] by the streams of water, ready to bring forth its fruit in its season; its leaf also shall not fade or wither; and everything he does shall prosper [and come to maturity].*

—Psalm 1:1–3 (AMP)

*A* real man carries significant responsibility and is aware of the charge given to him as a man of God, and he gladly embraces and satisfies his ongoing duty, which includes being a protector, lover, encourager and supporter, provider, and leader.

## 1. He is a PROTECTOR.

God is a protector, and because man is made in His image, he should be a protector too. Psalm 91:2–4 says, "He is my defender and protector. ... He will cover you with His wings; you will be safe in His care; His faithfulness will protect you and defend you."

You should always feel a strong sense of safety and security with your man—*always*. You should never feel intimidated or feel it is necessary to walk on eggshells. Ask yourself, *Is he a protector? Does he make every effort to keep me from harm and provide a covering under which I feel safe and secure? Am I afraid to be myself, share my thoughts, or oppose something he says or does?* It may be time to reevaluate the relationship if you are unable to say with 100 percent certainty that he is a protector and that he actively protects your spiritual, mental, physical, and emotional health. If you are committed to the relationship, however, you need to have some important discussions:

- Talk with him about your commitment, and reassure him that you are committed to working together to get the relationship on the right track.

- Share what God has revealed to you about the attributes of a godly relationship, and get his input about how he sees the two of you moving forward in a godly relationship.

- Listen to his definition of a godly relationship and see if it is aligned with the true meaning.

- Outline what each of you can do to have a relationship pleasing to the Father, and thereby to each other.

- Commit to change and to doing better.

- Pay attention to progress—or lack thereof—by journaling what you observe in the relationship. Compare your notes monthly and identify areas that have improved, are improving, or need improvement.

- By working together, you should see a positive transition in him from boy to man of God.

## 2. He is a LOVER.

He loves Jesus with all of his heart, which means he loves you with his whole heart too! Because he loves, his actions and attitude demonstrate that he is made in the image of God, by bearing the fruit of the Spirit.

- He walks in love with action and not just words.

- He would rather give than receive.

- He is kind and full of joy and peace, goodness, and faithfulness.

- He shares truth and shows mercy and grace.

- He practices self-control. Through the grace of Jesus, he controls his temper, sexual desires, at-risk or compromising behaviors, tongue, emotions, and negative actions.

The Gospels record a story of the loving action of a woman who anointed Jesus with an expensive perfume. Though their accounts are slightly different (Matthew 26, Mark 14, Luke 7, and John 12), all four Gospels show that a woman anointed Jesus with an expensive perfume and someone objected to the act of love. One important element to glean from the stories is that one person vocally expressed his disdain for the loving action because the seemingly more appropriate alternative was to sell the pricey perfume for financial gain. Jesus gently and lovingly reminded those around Him that the kindness displayed was done in love. The story shows us that even today, people may need a friendly reminder of what love looks like. Your man may need a gentle nudge regarding loving actions because he is imperfectly human and, as such, will fall short.

### 3. He is an ENCOURAGER/SUPPORTER.

Death and life are in the power of the tongue (Proverbs 18:21), meaning your man can destroy your spirit with what he says or can strengthen it. Your man should consider it joy to speak life to you and constantly support your happiness, joy, overall health, goals, and so much more. He chooses his words wisely and uses them in a way that promotes growth and excellence in you and the relationship, and he steers clear of strife and negative influence. Your man also provides encouragement in enriching your walk with Jesus and actively supports the two of you embarking upon the journey to a godly relationship.

God gave men and women different abilities and gifts to support each other, especially in the union of marriage: "Two are better than one because they have a good return for their labor. For if either of them falls, the one will lift up his companion. But woe to the one who falls when there is not another to lift him up" (Ecclesiastes 4:9–10). If you encounter a challenge, your man's role is to provide whatever you need to feel better and move ahead. If he discourages you and blames you for what happened, it is an indicator that he has evil stored up: "A good man brings good things out of the good stored up in him, and an evil man brings evil things out of the evil stored up in him" (Matthew 12:35).

### 4. He is a PROVIDER.

First Timothy (5:8) says, "Anyone who does not provide for their relatives, and especially for their own household, has denied the faith and is worse than an unbeliever." When you become one with your man as husband and wife, he thinks about you and your needs and works to ensure that you are taken care of. He will work more than one job if necessary, but he does not sit around waiting for the perfect job while you take care of him. He will work hard to provide hous ing, food, transportation, education, and the like. It is neither burdensome nor bothersome for him to work hard for you, because this is what real men do. Of course, women can take care of themselves and can contribute to the household, but a man recognizes and honors his role in providing for his family.

## 5. He is a LEADER.

Following your man should not be a scary endeavor! You should confidently be able to trust him to make wise decisions because he is a man of integrity rooted in the Lord. When the Bible tells us that wives should submit to their husbands, it means when the husband's heart and spirit belong to the Most High. If your husband is of the world and serves his best interests, more than likely, he will not make wise decisions and you should not follow that worldliness. If you are married or in a relationship that could lead to marriage, ask yourself, *Do I trust that his spirit is of God and that his heart belongs to the Lord?* First Corinthians 11:3 reminds us: "But I want you to realize that the head of every man is Christ, and the head of the woman is man, and the head of Christ is God." If a husband leads well, his wife and children will be spiritually mature.

---

**You must know who you are in God before you are able to receive with confidence the man He has for you.**

---

It is very important to realize that God wants you and your man to flourish and thrive in your relationship. You cannot flourish in a relationship with a boy, only with a man of God. What a difference you will notice when you are in a committed relationship with someone who is committed to the Lord! Being in a relationship with a boy of the world in no way compares to the joy and fullness of being in a relationship with a real man!

A man honors God in deed and speech. He does not pretend to be something he is not, he does not cause harm, and he does not seek to elevate himself via you and your belongings. It is important to recognize deceivers and the adversary at work in your life. God wants you to be in a healthy, happy, and loving relationship with a real man. He wants you to be so in tune with who you are in Him that you will not accept the waywardness of boys pretending to be men any longer. You must know who you are in God before you are able to receive with confidence who and what He has in store for you. When your spirit alerts you to something from God, you must take action and not be complacent, accepting a relationship that is contrary to everything God is. You should not expect your man to be perfect, but you must require that he be a man of integrity who recognizes and treats you like the child of the Most High.

You have options in everything you do. You can choose to stay with a boy and please the world, or you can choose to follow God and please Him. In a counseling session, Nancy made a statement that I shall never forget: "If I had listened to and obeyed God months before when He told me to leave Keith, I truly believe that I would not have experienced the physical abuse and the constant emotional and mental abuse would have been short-lived. It is so important to listen to God and get out of these abusive relationships and stop thinking that these boys will change." I feel confident stating that if you listen, obey, and honor God, you will experience every blessing He has in store for you. You can do this by building a strong foundation of faith, love, and wisdom.

## Helpful Scriptures

"[For being as he is] a man of two minds (hesitating, dubious, irresolute), [he is] unstable and unreliable and uncertain about everything [he thinks, feels, decides]." (James 1:8 AMP)

"Do not let any unwholesome talk come out of your mouths, but only what is helpful for building others up according to their needs, that it may benefit those who listen. Get rid of all bitterness, rage and anger, brawling and slander, along with every form of malice. Be kind and compassionate to one another, forgiving each other, just as in Christ God forgave you." (Ephesians 4:29, 31–32)

"Be devoted to one another in love. Honor one another above yourselves." (Romans 12:10)

"Therefore encourage one another and build each other up, just as in fact you are doing." (1 Thessalonians 5:11)

"But if you are led by the Spirit, you are not under the law. The acts of the flesh are obvious: sexual immorality, impurity and debauchery; idolatry and witchcraft; hatred, discord, jealousy, fits of rage, selfish ambition, dissensions, factions and envy; drunkenness, orgies, and the like. I warn you, as I did before, that those who live like this will not inherit the kingdom of God. But the fruit of the Spirit is love, joy, peace, forbearance, kindness, goodness, faithfulness, gentleness and self-control. Against such things there is no law. Those who belong to Christ Jesus have crucified the flesh with its passions and desires. Since we live by the Spirit, let us keep in step with the Spirit." (Galatians 5:18–25)

"So God created mankind in His own image, in the image of God He created them; male and female He created them." (Genesis 1:27) Remember, everything God creates is good; therefore, you should be treated like a good thing!

## Activity

What words best describe the current man in your life?

_____

_____

_____

_____

_____

What words would you use to describe the last two men with whom you had relationships?

_____

_____

_____

_____

_____

What similarities do you notice in 1 and 2 above?

_____

_____

_____

_____

_____

Moving forward, when asked to describe the man in your new godly relationship, how will you respond…what will be some of his key characteristics?

_____

_____

_____

_____

_____

What words would you use to describe yourself now, and how do you *want* to describe yourself?

Your current description                    Your ideal description

_____          _____

_____          _____

_____          _____

_____          _____

_____          _____

Think of your current relationship. Are both of you giving your best? What would you like to change about your relationship to make it your best?

_____

_____

_____

_____

_____

Have the men in your previous relationships given their best? Do you notice similar traits and tendencies in the men you date?

_____

_____

_____

_____

_____

If you are currently in a relationship, what contributions are you making to ensure that it is a godly relationship?

_____

_____

_____

_____

_____

Would you want your daughter to act like you and do the same things you do if she were in a relationship? Why or why not? What effect could your current actions have on your daughter, niece, granddaughter?

_____

_____

_____

_____

_____

Would you be happy to see your daughter date someone like your current boyfriend or the last two or three you were in a relationship with? Why or why not? (Before answering, think about the traits of boys versus those of men.)

_____

_____

_____

_____

_____

## Prayer

Father, thank You for the opportunity to start making better decisions to do better! I have not always honored You as I should, and as I continue to grow in You, I pray for wisdom and the revelation to do better. I realize the importance of honoring You in my relationship and being honored by a godly man. Lord, I pray for forgiveness for relying on the world instead of You to dictate what happens in my relationships. I know that if I stay in You and honor Your commands, I will experience Your best, and I know nothing in the world can compare to what You do! I long to be closer to You, to hear You, and for You to be closer to me. I thank You that I am on my way to making better decisions and getting ready for the real man you have for me! Lord, I thank You for Your love, grace, and mercy and for another chance to get it right. I love You. In Jesus' name. Amen.

# III: LOVE, FAITH, AND WISDOM

*Therefore everyone who hears these words of mine and puts them
into practice is like a wise man who built his house on the rock.
The rain came down, the streams rose, and the winds blew and
beat against that house; yet it did not fall, because it had its foundation on the rock. But everyone who hears these words of mine
and does not put them into practice is like a foolish man who built
his house on sand. The rain came down, the streams rose, and
the winds blew and beat against that house, and it fell with a
great crash.*

—Matthew 7:24–27

*B*efore you start a relationship, or even while in a relationship, it is important to have a discussion with your man to determine if the two of
you have the same desire to move forward with a relationship built and based
on the Word of God as a strong foundation. As a counselor, I find that this critical
discussion is often discounted or neglected when two people decide to start a
relationship or when having difficulties in their relationship. To be able to repair
any cracks and to avoid a complete collapse, your relationship must have a solid
infrastructure established on the principles of love, faith, and wisdom.

# 7

# LOVE IS ESSENTIAL

*But the fruit of the Spirit is love, joy, peace, patience, kindness,*
*goodness, faithfulness, gentleness, self-control; against such things*
*there is no law.*

—Galatians 5:22

*T*he first offspring of the Spirit is love. Did you know you are charged to love everyone? It is not a coincidence that love is the primary principle. The importance of love to God is clear throughout the Bible: "For God so loved the world that He gave His only begotten Son" (John 3:16); "Love your neighbor as you love yourself" (Mark 12:31); and "Love does no harm to a neighbor" (Romans 13:10).

When you and your man truly know and understand what love is, you desire to be better, because Jesus is love. Love is the very foundation that every relationship, both personal and professional, should be based on; it is at the heart of everything. I pray that by the time you have finished this book, the Spirit will have moved in a mighty way and you will truly know what it means to be loved by your mate, to love your mate, and to have a relationship that is inspired by and honors Jesus.

We know that there are different types of love, but the love of Jesus that I reference is agape, the type of love that you have been called to show and to share with everyone. In English, we use only one word for love, but in Greek, there are different types of love, including storge (*storgē*), agape (*agápē*), eros (*érōs*), and philia. When God says to love your neighbors, including your enemies, he is referring to agape, which is the love of God for man and the love of man for God; agape is the standard for loving everyone. Then, as you create or develop relationships, you engage in other types of love. For example, when someone has children, the parent and child experience storge, which is love and affection felt between parents and children. When you are married, you experience eros, which is intimate love and sexual passion, and philia is love shared between friends.

When you are in a relationship or being pursued for the purposes of starting a relationship, the man pursuing you is charged to love (agape) you. I have learned over the years that the definition of love is relative to individuals. Even though Jesus makes clear what love is required of everyone, men and women in relationships often have contrasting definitions. In couples' counseling sessions, the involved parties are usually not on the same page in defining love and demonstrating what love looks like in relationships.

First Corinthians 13:4–8a is one of many well-known passages that introduce us to the meaning of love: "Love is patient, love is kind. It does not envy, it does not boast, it is not proud. It does not dishonor others, it is not self-seeking, it is not easily angered, it keeps no record of wrongs. Love does not delight in evil but rejoices with truth. It always protects, always trusts, always hopes, always perseveres. Love never fails." Is this your definition of love? Did you know that this is how love should look in your relationship and that this is what your man should joyfully bring to you daily? The love from your man, or the man who is pursuing you, should be nothing short of this biblical definition.

---

## What does love look like to you? Are you being 1 Corinthians loved?

---

The first section of 1 Corinthians 13—specifically verses 1–3—reveals that you may be able to do great things like speak in tongues, prophesy, understand all mysteries, have faith that moves mountains, and give all you have to those in need, but if you do not have love, you are nothing, have nothing, and gain nothing. Love is the most important part of manhood. When a man knows the love of Jesus and offers that love to you, he puts you first; his intention is not to damage you but to 1 Corinthians love you. He knows that death and life are in the power of the tongue (Proverbs 18:21a), and he knows how to speak with you without being offensive, hurtful, or verbally abusive. He is thoughtful, considers how his actions and words will affect you, and seeks guidance from the Father when he feels a situation or conversation is not headed in the right direction. Are you being 1 Corinthians loved?

In a previous relationship, my man and I had discussions about the importance of 1 Corinthians love. For Christmas, I presented him a leather Bible; my inscription in it read something along the lines of us loving each other with 1 Corinthians love and having God's Word as the foundation of our relationship. Unfortunately, because he was the Pretender, he publicly declared a 1 Corinthians love in our relationship but his actions were completely contrary to love. He underestimated the relevance of Scripture and did not abide by the Word as he professed to.

Verses 15–17 of 1 John 4 say, "Whoever confesses that Jesus is the Son of God, God abides in him, and he in God. And we have known and believed the love that God has for us. God is love, and he who abides in love abides in God, and God in him. Love has been perfected among us in this: that you may have boldness in the day of judgment; because as He is, so are we in this world." This text lets you know that God resides in whoever confesses that Jesus is the Son of God. It confirms that, with your genuine confession, He is in you and that you are united in God. In some Bible translations, the term "dwell" is used instead of abide, but it still means to inhabit, to live as a resident, to reside, to live in a specified place, or to remain. You abide or dwell in God, and He in you. This reflects a core component of your relationship with Him, in that you are united with Him. God expects a man to abide in love, thereby abiding in Him.

This means that when trouble or challenges arise in the relationship, your man responds and handles the situation in love. He does not become physically abusive. He does not think he is validated to practice infidelity. He does not use it as an opportunity to lash out and disrespect you verbally. Instead, he handles the situation as a man of God: perhaps he takes a few minutes to manage his emotions before attempting to bring resolution to the situation; maybe he asks you to take a few moments to calm your emotions and then return to have a conversation when you are in a state allowing the two of you to work together to resolve the issue; or maybe he tells you what the resolution is going to be and you affirmatively acknowledge his authority because you trust the God in him.

---

**A man of God has the authority to handle relational challenges, and you should acknowledge that authority because you trust the God in him.**

---

The text of 1 John shines a bright light on the relationship that a man of God should have with Him: the closest relationship that someone can have with another, and what God wants to have with both your man and you. To abide in someone means to be inseparable from that person; when someone abides in God, God is with that person all the time and is a part of that person, and that person is a part of Him. God's love is perfect, and although your man's love is imperfect, he should make every effort to 1 Corinthians love you and to bring the God who abides to your relationship. Verses 5–6 of 1 John 2 are a good cross-reference Scripture for abiding in God: "But if anyone obeys His Word, love for

God is truly made complete in them. This is how we know we are in Him: Whoever claims to live in Him must live as Jesus did."

What does love look like when you are in a relationship? What evidence demonstrates that he loves (agape) you? Remember, no matter what phase of the relationship you are in, agape love should be evident in your husband, boyfriend, fiancé, or suitor; it should *always* be there and will reveal itself in these ways:

- Respect

- Patience

- Honorable

- Compassion

- Integrity

- Kindness

- Self-control

- A reflection of the image of God

As the woman in the relationship, you should see evidence of God residing in your man's loving actions, faith, and words. Take a moment to reflect on the evidence you see, or do not see, that God resides in him. Write it down and determine if it is obvious that Jesus dwells in him.

It does not look like:

- Sex (unless married)

- Abuse (physical, verbal, or emotional)

- Dishonesty or deceitfulness

- Ungodly character

- Anger or rage

- Self-indulgence

- Game playing

With Jesus as the model, love looks the same for everyone. Love does not do anything that would cause harm. A man's job is to bring joy, peace, security, and compassion—not hurt, disrespect, feelings of insecurity or inadequacy, or distress, because they are not a part of love. If you find that you regularly experience these things that are not part of love, your significant other is not abiding in Jesus or love and it is time to evaluate the foundation of your relationship. A one-time offense of truly accidental misconduct is not an omission of love, but *regular* and *repetitive* acts of cheating, lying, and/or being duplicitous are not loving: "If we deliberately keep on sinning after we have received the knowledge of the truth, no sacrifice for sins is left" (Hebrews 10:26).

If your significant other is encouraging sexual intercourse and you are not married, he is not showing godly love; however, if he respects you by watching how he speaks to you, constantly demonstrating his integrity, keeping your best interests at heart, participating calmly in disagreements, and making decisions that entertain the two of you rather than just himself, he is exuding the love of Jesus. What does he do?

It is important, as you live a life pleasing to God, to take time to evaluate yourself, your relationship, and your man or potential man. Having God's input and following His direction is critical to your future and achieving your purpose. God wants the best for you, and so do I.

Matthew 22:39 says, "Love your neighbor as yourself." This Scripture also calls for you to love yourself in the same way as you love your neighbor. Romans 13:10 says, "Love does no harm to a neighbor." This confirms that you are to protect yourself and to not stay anywhere that will cause you harm. Keep in mind that harm can be physical, emotional, spiritual, or mental. If it causes harm, it is not part of love and needs to be removed from the relationship. If that cannot be done, it is time for you to remove yourself from the relationship, because you are to be loved! I understand that this may be easier said than done, but it can be done. Your perfect Father would not instruct you on how to be treated if those instructions were not possible to fulfill. He does not say love is only sometimes, that you should be loved only when things are going well, or that you should be loved when your man gets the promotion, or when you are in public. Love is always love.

In John 13:34–35, Jesus says, "A new command I give you: Love one another. As I have loved you, so you must love one another. By this, everyone will know that you are my disciples, if you love one another." This powerful quote from

Jesus confirms that you are to be intentionally loved. A Christian man actively shows the love of God to his woman, and as his woman, you should know with 100 percent certainty that he loves you because of his actions. Everyone should know the same by his actions—including his boys who encourage him to get another woman's phone number, flirt with another woman, go to a gentlemen's club, or even have an affair. His friends should see that he is a man of God who vehemently denounces such behavior and actions because of His love for Jesus and you.

---

**For you to identify and receive the love of a real man, you must love yourself: "Love your neighbor as yourself" (Matthew 22:39; my emphasis)**

---

Because God instructs us that love is foremost, the adversary will try to make you believe it is not as important as He says. Do not fall for that trap and stay in a relationship that mocks the love of God. The devil's purpose is to kill, steal, and destroy (John 10:10) everything about you: kill your spirit, destroy your relationship with God, steal your amazing future, and steal the possibility of you ever having a loving relationship with the man God has for you. Nothing would give the devil more pleasure than to interrupt or hinder God's plan for your life. This is another reason you and your man must stay in the Word and have a solid foundation on which to build your relationship.

Today, you and your man should stand firm in the foundation and let satan know, through your actions, that you are standing strong and resisting his evil temptations. The only way that will happen is if you and your man study your Word daily and spend time with God. Talk with Him, share with Him, and know Him. The devil's only purpose is to destroy you because he is the epitome of evil…d-evil, but God's purpose is to give you life more abundantly. The devil knows exactly what buttons to push to get you to go against the perfect will for your life. What will you do? Will you allow satan to interfere with the perfect purpose, or will you be strong and courageous and defeat the devil through the power of the Spirit that dwells within, allowing your man to lead you on a faith-filled path?

Are you currently or have you ever been in a relationship in which lying, cheating, abuse, deceit, or other evil occurred regularly? A man will not bring this into a relationship because he fears the Lord, takes his relationship with Christ seriously, knows who he is in Christ, and knows his role in the relationship.

Check any of the ways below that a man in your life has shown his "love" to you:

_____ hit you

_____ pushed you

_____ lied to you

_____ engaged in inappropriate relationships

_____ committed adultery

_____ used you to move himself ahead (self-promotion)

_____ put your health at risk by having sex with another woman

_____ engaged in inappropriate communication with other women

_____ put his interests above yours

_____ verbally abused you

_____ caused you emotional and mental distress, and/or abused you emotionally and mentally

_____ downplayed your relationship with Christ or denied the need for Christ in the relationship

Loving everyone means not just your family and friends, but also the passersby on the street. The homeless person asking for money or food. Your ex from the relationship that ended poorly. Even if your current mate treats you poorly, you are to love him. (Love does not mean staying in a relationship and taking the abuse, however; you can love him safely and from afar.) The law of love is unchanging: We do not get to pick and choose whom we love or how we love but are to share and show the love of Jesus to everyone.

It does not matter if others do not return the sentiment/action; regardless of how others behave, love must be a driving force in what your man does—and in what you do—and, it is important that you can see this in him. Observe how he treats strangers in need, the family member who is a struggling single parent, his ex, or, if he has one, the mother of his child. Your observations will allow you to see what is in his heart.

We say, "I love you," to our significant others when we wake up in the morning and before we go to bed at night, at the end of a telephone call, or on our way to work in the morning. But have you ever stopped to think what love really looks like? Have you asked yourself, *Am I really loving this person? And is he really loving me?*

I remember counseling Nancy and Keith in the early- to mid-phase of their relationship. She asked him, "Do you love me?" and he answered yes. Her follow-up inquiry was "Why don't you ever say it?" He responded, "Because if I say it, I want to make sure I will live up to it." Soon thereafter, he told her he loved her, and in her mind, that meant he was living up to it; to him, it was just another facet of being a Pretender. He was engaged in many inappropriate side relationships with other women as he shared those words with her.

In Romans 13:8–10, God expounds on love: "Let no debt remain outstanding, except the continuing debt to love one another, for whoever loves others has fulfilled the law. The commandments, 'You shall not commit adultery,' 'You shall not murder,' 'You shall not steal,' 'You shall not covet,' and whatever other command there may be, are summed up in this one command: Love your neighbor as yourself.' Love does no harm to a neighbor. Therefore love is the fulfillment of the law." This Scripture provides support to the idea that Keith was unable to love himself and was thereby unable to love Nancy or Jesus. If you love your neighbor as yourself and love does no harm to a neighbor, then love does no harm to self. Keith harmed himself with his actions, which caused harm to his spirit; spiritual self-harm is extremely damaging.

Do not allow the adversary to cause you to deviate from your path. Keith was able to deceive almost everyone he knew, including himself, into thinking he was a man who loved. Based on the world's definition of love that is self-serving, he believed he loved, but based on God's definition of love, he did not—he was not yet able to open his heart to accept and trust Jesus. Love is a verb, and it stems from having Jesus in your heart. Keith wanted to select those to whom he would show love, but that demonstrates blatant resistance to what God wants; God has made clear that we are to love everyone. In Nancy and Keith's relationship, Keith's actions were the opposite of love. Love produces the fruit of the spirit; if what someone calls love produces recurrent tears, grief, sadness, anger, and similar emotions, it is not love. In this case, Keith's inability to show love meant that he had not embraced the spirit of Jesus and did not trust God to do what He does best, which is to take care of every single detail of Keith's life.

---

**Causing harm to your spirit is spiritual self-harm and is extremely damaging.**

---

When a man welcomingly receives and embraces the transforming love of Jesus, he does not want to engage in the behavior he may have performed when he was a boy; he wants to be the light of Jesus in the carnal world. Part of loving and being loved, and of building your foundation, is knowing what voice is from satan and what voice is from God. Satan's voice will demolish and subdue you, but God's voice will lead you down the path of righteousness. What is your plan to ensure that you stay focused and on your God-given path to receive love from the man chosen just for you?

## Helpful Scriptures

"And now these three remain: faith, hope and love. But the greatest of these is love." (1 Corinthians 13:13)

"Dear friends, let us love one another, for love comes from God. Everyone who loves has been born of God and knows God." (1 John 4:7)

## Activity

How has this chapter changed your perception or thoughts of a loving relationship?

_____

_____

_____

_____

_____

Are you being 1 Corinthians loved in your relationship?

_____

_____

_____

_____

_____

Will knowing that God wants you to experience His love have an effect on your relationship in the future?

_____

_____

_____

_____

_____

## Prayer

 Thank You, Lord, for loving me. I feel that I have not always been truly loved in relationships the way You intend and desire for me, and I feel that I may not have loved myself the way I should. I am thankful to You for sharing what love looks like and how I should expect to be loved by the man You have chosen for me. Building a strong foundation starts with love, and I pray that You remove anything from me that is contrary to love and that You help me, along with my mate, to start building our foundation on this very important principle. Your Word says that love is patient, love is kind. It does not envy, it does not boast, it is not proud. It does not dishonor others, it is not self-seeking, it is not easily angered, it keeps no records of wrongs. Love does not delight in evil but rejoices with the truth. It always protects, always trusts, always hopes, always perseveres. By honoring Your Word and teachings, I am honoring the relationship You have blessed me to have. Anything that is contrary to love is contrary to Your will and is, thereby, evil. Help me to put love first, and thank You for blessing me with a man who does the same. In the name of Jesus, I pray. Amen.

# 8

# FAITH IS CRITICAL

*Lord, You are my God; I will exalt Your Name, for in perfect faithfulness you have done wonderful things, things planned long ago.*

—Isaiah 25:1

Putting your faith in God is probably one of the most difficult experiences you may encounter. Putting your faith in God is the pinnacle of difficulty when it comes to choosing your mate, because you want to be in charge of that. You are the only one who knows what you want and what is best for you, right? God says no. To put your faith in something you cannot see, touch, or hear seems too uncertain and leaves too much room for error. That is exactly what God wants you to do, however.

Psalm 143:8 says, "Let the morning bring me word of your unfailing love, for I have put my trust in you. Show me the way I should go, for to you I entrust my life." I love this Scripture because it speaks so much to the love God has for you and what trusting God really looks like. "Let the morning bring me word of your unfailing love, for I have put my trust in You" shows the psalmist's desire to be connected to the Lord, that he wakes up spending time with Him, and because of God's love, he can and does trust God. The next sentence—"Show me the way I should go, for to you I entrust my life"—speaks to the psalmist's complete trust in God for everything. The psalmist wants and seeks God to guide him in everything he does. He acknowledges that he is incapable of relying on self to make decisions and looks to God for guidance. In summary, these are the steps of the psalmist in relying on God for everything:

- He wakes up ready to spend time with the Lord and to enrich their relationship.

- He acknowledges that God's love is pure and perfect and has the psalmist's best interest at heart.

- He puts his trust in God because of God's love for him.

- He relies on God for all aspects of his life. He seeks God's will for his life before he gets started with his day.

- He releases any worry, anxiety, doubt, and uncertainty to God and believes God will wholly take care of him.

How did the psalmist get to the point of trusting God completely? "So faith comes from hearing, and hearing through the Word of Christ" (Romans 10:17). Studying His Word and developing an intimate relationship with Him will strengthen your faith. Going through experiences and knowing that God will never leave you nor forsake you (Deuteronomy 31:6) also strengthens your faith. Deuteronomy 31:8 reiterates God's faithfulness to you: "The LORD is the one who goes ahead of you; He will be with you. He will not fail you or forsake you. Do not fear or be dismayed." I can write about faith all day, but you have to experience it for yourself and become intimate with God; you must know Him as He reveals Himself to you in His Word.

When you make carnal decisions based on self, you do not trust God to be who He is: the perfect, all-knowing God who always does what He says He will do. In every aspect of life, especially your relationship, faith in God is critical. Faith, as defined by Merriam-Webster, means (1) complete trust or confidence in someone or something and (2) strong belief in God or in the doctrines of a religion, based on spiritual apprehension rather than proof. When you rely on self to make relational decisions without the Word of God, you let God know that you do not trust Him to send you the right person, that you do not believe He knows what you need or want, and that you know better than He does. Is that the message you want to send?!

When God says in Jeremiah 29:11, "For I know the plans I have for you, plans to prosper and not to harm you, plans to give you hope and a future," He means it. He is not just talking about one component of your life; He is concerned with every life dynamic there is, including your mate and every single relational component, even sex. God is concerned with your sex life when you get married. When we go back to the beginning, in Genesis, we see He made woman specifically for man. This confirms that you have a divinely selected mate. God made you for somebody, but you have to be patient and have faith that he will be delivered: "Now faith is the substance of things hoped for, the evidence of things not seen" (Hebrews 11:1, KJV).

Trusting God means not relying on the natural sense of what you see to understand what is happening or to predict the outcome. It means knowing without a doubt that God is working things out for your good. On the outside, your challenging situations may appear uncertain or bleak, but you must remember that God is a problem solver, a fixer, and always has your best interests at heart. Think about earthly relationships: When you do not trust that someone will keep their word, you make alternate arrangements or have a backup plan to make sure the need is satisfied. When you know that your colleague is always late to work and puts your deadlines at risk, for example, you may adjust your work schedule and get to work earlier to ensure the successful completion of the assignment. When you do not trust that your relative knows how to fix the plumbing challenge in your home, a plumber may surprisingly show up at the same time to fix the leak. We have all experienced moments when we did not trust a person to do what he/she promised and took matters into our own hands. When God instructs you to do things a certain way but you do not do them in that way, you are essentially laughing in His face and making the bold statement that you do not trust Him and you can do it better. When you do not trust or have faith in someone, the relationship is superficial at best. A lack of trust impedes any relational progress because you feel that you are unable to count on this individual. It is the same with God. If you believe in your ability to get things done, rather than believing in God, He cannot trust you with information or the specific plans He has for you.

God requires faith, and without it, there is no relationship. When you are in a faith-filled relationship with God, He shares things with you because He is able to trust you in your faithfulness. In Genesis 12, God trusted the faith of Abram and told him to move to an undisclosed location. Abram did what he was told. Because God trusted Abram, He shared secrets with and made promises to Abram. For example, God told Abram that he would conceive a child with his wife, Sarai, and promised to make him the father of many nations (Genesis 17). God then changed Abram's name to Abraham as confirmation of the covenant. Jesus is a descendant of Abraham, and the covenant was fulfilled.

Another example comes from the sixth chapter of Joshua. God trusted Joshua and let him know that He would deliver Jericho into Joshua's hands. God instructed Joshua to walk around the city once a day for six days and that on the seventh day, to walk around the city with his army seven times and, on the seventh time, blow their horns. God told Joshua the wall around the city would fall and Joshua and his army would be able to charge the city and take it over. Joshua did exactly as he was told, and God's promise to him was fulfilled.

In another instance, God trusted Mary (the mother of Jesus) because Mary trusted Him. Mary really had to have faith in God to have a baby conceived through the

Holy Spirit, because of everything she could possible endure as a result, including the possibility of being stoned because she was unwed and pregnant, people considering her a woman of lust, and Joseph ending the relationship and leaving her. But Mary was ready and obliged to be a vessel for the Lord's work and give birth to our Savior, a descendant of David who was a descendant of Abraham. There are many examples of faith in the Bible, and it is good to be reminded of them, but ultimately, you have to be willing to experience faith for yourself.

Keep in mind that you will have trials as you develop your relationship with God and strengthen your faith, because the devil wants to keep you from doing that. He wants you to remain of the world because it solidifies his purpose to destroy you and take you from your path, ensuring your demise as you contribute to the demise of society. In 1 Peter 5:8, God instructs us to "be alert and of sober mind. Your enemy the devil prowls around like a roaring lion looking for someone to devour." Satan is looking to devour you and your family, relationships, peace, and joy. He wants you to do things that you are not supposed to do, things that remove you from the will of God. You have to tell the devil today that he is not going to destroy you because you are made in the image of God and follow the example of Jesus and not of the world.

When you are a woman of faith, it is important to have a man of faith. The importance of trusting God (believing) and of having faith (acting on His belief) is paramount to the success of the relationship. Your man's faith should be strongly evident, or he should be diligently working to get it to that point. God makes it clear that a man's actions must coincide with what he speaks. If he speaks of faith and fidelity, a man's actions should demonstrate the same. A man is a person of faith and deeds. If he speaks love, honor, and commitment, his actions will demonstrate such. He will bear the fruits of the spirit—love, joy, peace, patience, kindness, goodness, faithfulness, gentleness, and self-control—and each will be evident in his actions. He will put you first and will deny selfish ambition. He will control his temper and will fully embrace patience and kindness as gifts from God. If he sees the Jesus in you, when he says, "I love you," he will not do what is contrary to God's definition of love. God wants to use you and your man to show the world the good fruits that are produced through a loving and faithful relationship. This calls for him (and you too) to believe and act in faith that Jesus is Lord and that God is omnipotent, omnipresent, omniscient, and omnibenevolent.

## Helpful Scriptures

"Trust in the Lord with all your heart and lean not on your own understanding; in all your ways submit to Him and He will make your paths straight." (Proverbs 3:5–6)

"Commit to the LORD whatever you do, and he will establish your plans." (Proverbs 16:3)

"But blessed is the one who trusts in the LORD, whose confidence is in him. They will be like a tree planted by the water that sends out its roots by the stream. It does not fear when heat comes; its leaves are always green. It has no worries in a year of drought and never fails to bear fruit." (Jeremiah 17:7–8)

"May the God of hope fill you with all joy and peace as you trust in him, so that you may overflow with hope by the power of the Holy Spirit." (Romans 15:13)

## Activity

Do you believe that when you follow God's instruction, God blesses you with the best possible outcome? Try the faith activities below.

List three areas in which you lack faith in your romantic relationship. Explain why you feel you do not trust God to rule in these areas. (Do you believe that God's ways are best for you? If so, it is time to rely on Him and let Him have control of your life.)

_____

_____

_____

_____

_____

What steps will you take to trust and have faith in God in the areas listed above?

_____

_____

_____

_____

_____

If you believe your relationship is not a godly one, please list the reasons why and then list what you feel are the best options to change this so the two of you can enjoy the fruits of having a godly relationship. Keep in mind, prayer is always the best place to start, along with open and honest communication with your man.

_____

_____

_____

_____

_____

How will you approach making the necessary changes in your relationship? Below are some suggestions for beginning a conversation with your man.

- Share the effect that the ungodly behavior is having on you, and ask him how he feels about having an ungodly relationship.

- Discuss your desire to have a godly relationship and what a godly relationship looks like.

- Work with him to create a plan for both of you to follow to support having a godly relationship. For example, if one thing you would like to change is the strife regularly brought into the relationship by making harmful and hurtful statements, you may want to start with the guided tips below.

- ○ It is important for both parties to understand that poorly chosen words used in discussions or disagreements can cause long-term challenges and create unwanted discord. It is also important to know what God says about this topic.

  - □ Verses 3–5 of 1 Timothy shares that "if anyone teaches another doctrine and disagrees with the sound words of our Lord Jesus Christ and with godly teaching, he is conceited and understands nothing. Instead, he has an unhealthy interest in controversies and semantics, out of which come envy, strife, abusive talk, evil suspicions, and constant friction between men of depraved mind who are devoid of the truth. These men regard godliness as a means of gain."

  - □ "Drive out the mocker and out goes strife; quarrels and insults are ended." (Proverbs 22:10)

  - □ "A hot-tempered man stirs up strife, but he who is slow to anger quiets contention." (Proverbs 15:18)

  - □ "Let your conversation always be full of grace, seasoned with salt, so that you may know how to answer everyone." (Colossians 4:6)

  - □ "Those who consider themselves religious and yet do not keep a tight rein on their tongues deceive themselves, and their religion is worthless." (James 1:26)

  - □ "What goes into someone's mouth does not defile them, but what comes out of their mouth, that is what defiles them." (Matthew 15:11)

- ○ You and your man should discuss how both of you feel after reading the relevant Scripture and how you feel when you have contentious discussions.

- ○ Return to the last conversation the two of you had that incorporated a few of those hurtful or harmful comments, and discuss specific better ways to handle challenges in the future. What will you do when one or both of you feels the urge to say something that is not loving? How will you communicate that you need a moment to yourself to calm down?

- ○ Remember that if a conversation starts to get heated, it is okay to have the discussion later when both parties are ready to calmly talk.

- ○ Pray. Pray for healing and forgiveness. Pray to avoid falling into the trap of the enemy. Pray for strength, courage, and wisdom. Pray for each other and that the love of God will consume each of you.

- Discuss options that the two of you can use to support each other.

- If one (or both) of you slips and falls short, write down what happened, how it made both parties feel, and a better way of handling it in the future, then discuss when both of you are ready.

## Prayer

Lord, I need You. I have not always put my faith in You, and I regularly make decisions without seeking Your guidance. You have made Yourself available to 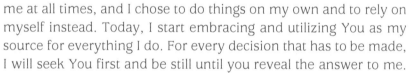 me at all times, and I chose to do things on my own and to rely on myself instead. Today, I start embracing and utilizing You as my source for everything I do. For every decision that has to be made, I will seek You first and be still until you reveal the answer to me. I am committed to spending more time with You and studying Your Word because faith comes by hearing the Word of God and I want that intimate relationship with You! I believe that every word You spoke is true and that with those words, I can stand in faith, knowing that You have a perfect plan for me and want only the best for me. Thank You, Lord, for never leaving me. I love You. In Jesus' name I pray. Amen.

# 9

# WISDOM IS NECESSARY

*But the wisdom that comes from heaven is first of all pure; then peace-loving, considerate, submissive, full of mercy and good fruit, impartial and sincere.*

—James 3:17

*W* isdom is another of God's amazing gifts to His children. Before we go on, though, let's take a moment to look at the common definition of wisdom. Merriam-Webster defines wisdom as (1) knowledge that is gained by having many experiences in life; (2) the natural ability to understand things that most other people cannot understand; and (3) knowledge of what is proper or reasonable: good sense or judgment.

Though those definitions have some accuracy, they are only partially true. I have made a few corrections to the above definitions to improve their accuracy and validity:

- Knowledge that is *received from God to apply to life's experiences*

- The *super*natural ability to understand things that most other people cannot understand

- Knowledge of what is proper or reasonable: good sense or judgment *that is given by God*

I agree that through the many experiences we encounter, our gift of wisdom is enriched, but that is not the original source of your wisdom. "The fear of the Lord is the beginning of knowledge, but fools despise wisdom and instruction" (Proverbs 1:7). I appreciate how the Benson Commentary explains this Scripture:

*The fear of the Lord*—That is, reverence for and obedience to God; *is the beginning of knowledge*—The foundation and source of it; without which all other knowledge is vain and useless. Mark well this sentence, reader: all wisdom, which is not founded in religion, in the true and genuine fear of God, is empty and unprofitable, and will be found such in the time of affliction, in the hour of death, and at the day of judgment. *But fools*—Wicked men, or men devoid of true religion, called fools throughout this whole book, *despise wisdom and instruction*—Are so far from attaining it, that they despise it, and all the means of getting it. (http://biblehub.com/commentaries/proverbs/1-7.htm)

When you love, know, and ask God for wisdom, you receive this gift. Wisdom is necessary for you and for the man of God. It helps you to discern the enemy's traps, leads you down a path of righteousness, offers protection, and prepares a path for you to receive blessings. In Proverbs 2:6, God reveals, "For the LORD gives wisdom; from His mouth come knowledge and understanding." Understanding and knowing how to mitigate challenges, make right choices, and love in the midst of everything you face are skills that you master only when you have wisdom. When we lack wisdom, do not fear or know God, ugly thoughts may intrude to promote even uglier actions and doors are opened for the enemy to come in and prompt us to do things we otherwise would not do. A Scripture that supports this is Proverbs 29:11: "Fools give full vent to their rage, but the wise bring calm in the end."

The Bible mentions wisdom and the ramifications of the lack thereof several times. People who lack wisdom are considered fools, foolish, or full of folly— not very godly or desirable traits. Lacking wisdom is the antithesis of being a godly man. If you notice that your man is unable to consistently demonstrate wise decision making, you may want to take a closer look at the dynamics of the relationship and the man. Folly is not just acting in a way that calls blatant attention to oneself but is also making poor decisions and relying on self to make things happen. When your man receives the gift of wisdom, he receives the knowledge to act in a godly manner, which is evident when he speaks and when he handles even the most delicate situations.

Proverbs 12:23 demonstrates the actions of the foolish: "Wise men don't make a show of their knowledge, but fools broadcast their foolishness." Can you recall multiple times when your man broadcast his foolishness for others to see? Maybe it was only in front of you, but his foolishness was clear. Perhaps it was in a disagreement that led to an act of anger or regret; maybe it was not trusting the Father in a situation and making a foolish decision; or perhaps the foolishness was ignoring the Word of God and believing in self to make it through the circumstance ahead.

The wise man brings peace, calm, and love to situations, whereas the fool promotes anger, rage, and separation. Your man should bring peace and calm and should discourage anger and rage in the relationship; he should do his best to keep strife out and to promote an environment of safety and security. He will not always be perfect, but he should try in every scenario to create a harmonious atmosphere, and when he does fall short, he should be able to acknowledge his mistake and ask forgiveness of God and you. Proverbs 23:9 reminds us that reasoning with fools is often a waste of effort: "Don't waste your breath on fools, for they will despise the wisest advice." If you are with a man who has not yet been gifted with wisdom, you may find it difficult to have an accomplished discussion with him, at which point it may be best to take time to pray and process. It could be that both of you lack wisdom and that you decide to work together to become who God has created you to be. If he has no desire to be a man of God, however, it is time to shake yourself loose. Wisdom is directly related to knowing God.

---

**When we lack wisdom and the heart to know God, doors are opened for the enemy to come in and prompt us to do things we otherwise would not do.**

---

Therefore everyone who hears these words of mine and puts them into practice is like a wise man who built his house on the rock. The rain came down, the streams rose, and the winds blew and beat against that house; yet it did not fall, because it had its foundation on the rock. But everyone who hears these words of mine and does not put them into practice is like the foolish man who built his house on the sand. The rain came down, the streams rose, and the winds blew and beat against that house, and it fell with a great crash. (Matthew 7:24–27)

In the above Scripture, God clearly shares the outcome for the wise man versus the fool. When the wise man comes against the torrential downpour of life's formidable challenges, he will withstand it and will remain standing! The fool, in contrast, will sink. He has nothing on which to stand or survive the ferocious storms of life.

The wise man does not build his foundation on the what-ifs of life:

- His job…what happens if he does not get that promotion?

- His wealth…what happens if it disappears?

- His looks…what happens if they fail?

- Who he knows…what happens if they disappear or cut him off?

- His status or presumed power…what happens if it is taken away?

God's Word transforms and changes everyone, and you should see your man becoming better in many areas as he comes to know God. His love should become more evident in his actions, his faith should be observably strengthened, and his wisdom should be recognizable in his decision making. Your faith, love, and wisdom will ensure your immovable footing in your relationship and otherwise. The two of you may bend and sway when the storms of life come, but you will not break or snap. Make the decision today, if you have not already, to trust and believe everything God has written. Make a conscientious effort to put others first and to love and seek Him in everything and with every decision.

## Helpful Scriptures

"All Scripture is God-breathed and is useful for teaching, rebuking, correcting and training in righteousness, so that the servant of God may be thoroughly equipped for every good work." (2 Timothy 3:16–17)

"My son, if you receive my words and treasure up my commandments with you, making your ear attentive to wisdom and inclining your heart to understanding; yes, if you call out for insight and raise your voice for understanding, if you seek it like silver and search for it as for hidden treasures, then you will understand the fear of the Lord and find the knowledge of God." (Proverbs 2:1–5)

"Make me to know your ways, O Lord; teach me your paths. Lead me in your truth and teach me, for you are the God of my salvation; for you I wait all the day long." (Psalm 25:4–5, ESV)

"Wisdom will save you from the ways of wicked men, from men whose words are perverse, who have left the straight paths to walk in dark ways, who delight in doing wrong and rejoice in the perverseness of evil, whose paths are crooked and who are devious in their ways." (Proverbs 2:12–15)

## Activity

Ask yourself the following questions and write your answers in the space provided.

Do I fear the Lord? How do I know that I do or do not? What actions demonstrate my fear of the Lord...or lack thereof?

_____

_____

_____

_____

## Prayer

 Lord, Your Word has opened my eyes to an area in my life that I truly lacked: fear of the Lord. I thank You for these words, and I pray that as I seek You first, You will give me the gift of wisdom in my relationship and situations I face daily. Lord, I confess there have been times when I was more concerned with folly than with wisdom, and I ask for Your forgiveness. Thank You for forgiveness! I am not proud of those moments, but I am going to use this new chance You have given me to put You first and follow Your desire for me and my life. As I keep my mind and heart set on You, I pray that Your spirit will consume me and Your wisdom will abound in my life so I can be a blessing to others and to myself by making better decisions that are aligned with Your Word. Your wisdom will allow me and the man You have for me to build the necessary solid foundation for our relationship. Thank You for removing the covering from my eyes and for letting me see Your light. I love You. In Jesus' name I pray. Amen.

# IV: POWER UP!

*Be on your guard; stand firm in the faith; be courageous; be strong. Do everything in love.*

—1 Corinthians 16:13–14

s you begin this final section of the book, I pray that you have a better understanding of all that God wants for you and your relationship:

- Trusting God and having faith

- Being strong in your faith, and unafraid to stand up and do what is right

- Loving God and yourself

- Being wise to the plans of the adversary to destroy you and your relationship with God

- Being loved by a man created just for you

It is also important for you to be aware of some key components regarding your role as you walk in your divine purpose, strengthen your faith, and become a better you! That is the focus of this section.

# 10

# YOUR ROLE

*Charm is deceptive, and beauty is fleeting; but a woman who fears the Lord is to be praised.*

—Proverbs 31:30 (NIV)

God has great plans for you: to "prosper you and not to harm you" (Jeremiah 29:11). This includes every detail of your life. He knows the number of hairs on your head (Matthew 10:30), which indicates that He cares and is concerned about who you will spend your life with. He is so invested that He has already determined the person for you and outlined the qualities and traits of your noble and honorable man. Your role is significant in having the godly relationship that is destined for greatness. It is critical that your man be a man of God, but it is also important that you be a woman of God. According to Genesis 2:21–24:

> So the Lord God caused the man to fall into a deep sleep; and while he was sleeping, he took one of the man's ribs and then closed up the place with flesh. Then the Lord God made a woman from the rib he had taken out of the man, and he brought her to the man. The man said, "This is now bone of my bones and flesh of my flesh; she shall be called 'woman,' for she was taken out of man." That is why a man leaves his father and mother and is united to his wife, and they become one flesh."

A woman of God in a relationship or looking to be in a relationship has been called to be upstanding and virtuous. The most important thing that you bring to the relationship is inward beauty—your heart and spirit. The Lord made you directly from man; that speaks to the significance of your special connection with the man God made just for you. Your connection is not significant with any male figure but is specific to whom God destined to be your lifelong mate. Proverbs 31:25–26 says a virtuous woman "is clothed with strength and dignity; she can laugh at the days to come. She speaks with wisdom, and faithful instruction is on her tongue." You have strength to withstand temptation, to live a life pleasing to God, and to stand firm in faith. Your dignity is recognized by your man and ensures that you receive the respect you are warranted. You are wise because you know and fear the Lord and have a relationship with Him, and you bless others with your wisdom.

Being a godly woman should be evident in everything you do, from the way you interact with strangers to the way you treat your man. The way you carry yourself and represent who you are is vital. Do not try to pretend to be someone you are not, but genuinely be a caring, loving, compassionate, and kind woman in every scenario. There will be times when frustration surfaces and your response may fall a little short, but that is okay. Remember that it is important to have a pure heart and a genuine desire to share the love of God in situations because you know that sharing His love will prompt others to do the same. Remember, people are always watching and observing how you react and respond, and often, what you do will engage them to mimic you and your actions.

Sharing these words reminds me of when I attended my cousin's high school graduation. It was a very special occasion filled with excitement and joy! As we were exiting the sardine-can-like parking lot with no traffic directors, I was trying to pull out of a parking space into the line of exiting traffic. The lady who had the option of letting me in (or not) decided to pull close enough to the car in front of her, almost hitting the car, to keep me from entering the parade of cars trying to find their way to the main road. I did not get upset but thought how sad it must be to work so hard at being unpleasant rather than sharing a kind and loving gesture with someone else. As she gave me the most evil look, I said, "God bless you." I do not know this woman, and it could be that this was one of those times when she fell short or was having a bad day, though my spirit said otherwise. I understand everyone wanted to get out of there, but showing kindness is much better than letting evil win.

When you do not know the love of Jesus, evil takes over, even through something as simple as driving. The driver in this situation was not dignified; she got caught up in the small things and missed the opportunity to love and to be a blessing. I believe wisdom would have instructed her to show and share love.

Even in the small daily activities such as driving, walking, taking public transportation, grocery shopping, or going out to eat, it is important to be dignified and Christlike. How do you handle similar situations? Are you kind and agreeable or aggressively unpleasant?

Proverbs 4:23 reminds us that our hearts reveal who we are: "Above all else, guard your heart, for everything you do flows from it." What will people know about you from an interaction with you? Will they find you to be impatient, selfish, lacking common courtesy, or helpful, loving, and giving? Will people gravitate toward your generous spirit or stay clear of you for fear of your wicked tongue? If people stay clear because you lack godly characteristics, this is an area that should be brought to the forefront for emergency care! No matter where you are or what you are doing, people should be able to look at you and see love. Your man should know that with you, he has found a good thing…and good in every sense of the word: supportive, encouraging, kind and compassionate, generous, understanding, and slow to anger. He should know that you are a woman from God for him, the woman who should become his wife, and he should know that when you marry, you will be an amazing helpmate and lover, which God intended you to be. He should be able to trust you because of the God in you. How should this translate in relationship terms? First, your godly man should want a virtuous woman. He should desire to be with some-one who honors God by honoring herself and her body. This includes waiting until you are married to have sex.

## Waiting for Sex…What?!

I know, I know, but it is true: We are supposed to wait until marriage to have sex, though the majority of women and men do not agree with this concept. Part of having faith and trusting God is directly related to this pleasurable event. Do you trust God enough to not give in to temptation? It is not the easiest thing in the world to do. In fact, it can be a most challenging struggle—but you will be so much better off than if you were to engage in an act that God abhors.

I was once talking to an old friend who was coming to town, and we made plans to grab dinner and hang out. I remember being excited to see him because it had been more than ten years since we had last seen each other. My friend and I had a special type of relationship, and there was no doubt in my mind that if we were to get together for dinner, the specialness would soon show up. Within minutes of making plans with him, I received a devotional e-mail that said, "Flee from sexual immorality. All other sins a person commits are outside the body, but whoever sins sexually, sins against their own body" (1 Corinthians 6:18). Really, Lord? I said, "Okay, God, I get it." I realized the Lord was giving me a stern warning, and He continued to do so over the next three days, with daily devotional e-mails and Bible Verses delivered to my phone:

- **You have let go of the commands of God and are holding on to the traditions of men** (Mark 7:8). This Scripture helped me understand that I was taking a turn in the wrong direction and being wrongly psyched into thinking, even if just for a moment, that I could justify having dinner with my friend.

- "Teacher, which is the greatest commandment in the Law?" Jesus replied: "'Love the Lord your God with all your heart and with all your soul and with all your mind.' This is the first and greatest commandment. And the second is like it: 'Love your neighbor as yourself.' All the Law and the Prophets hang on these two commandments" (Matthew 22:36–40). Here I feel He was telling me that I was forgetting that I am to love Him first, and that means with a pure heart and spirit—which I clearly was not doing—and that I needed to get on with that!

- You say, "Food for the stomach and the stomach for food, and God will destroy them both." The body, however, is not meant for sexual immorality but for the Lord, and the Lord for the body (1 Corinthians 6:13). This one is self-explanatory.

- But among you there must not be even a hint of sexual immorality, or of any kind of impurity, or of greed, because these are improper for God's holy people" (Ephesians 5:3). The Lord has chosen me for greatness and to do great things, and I cannot put myself in a situation that could potentially cause an ungodly action or reaction.

After the third day of receiving such messages, I said, "Nicole, what are you doing?! Do you see how the adversary creeps in to remove you from the will of God?" This incident goes to show how cunning and crafty he is. He knew the temptation had to be in the form a certain person for me to even consider going out; then the feelings and memories started surfacing from many years ago and I started convincing myself that going on a harmless outing with an old friend was totally doable. It was doable, but the elements to making poor decisions were all there.

I started reading additional Scripture about sexual immorality, and then I thanked God for loving me so much that He would speak directly to me and remind me of who I am in Him, and of my responsibility as a woman of God. He did not want to see me fail, so for three days, He sent Scripture that He knew would get my attention! Amazing!

Needless to say, I canceled the dinner—but that situation reminded me how loving and amazing God is. He wants you to succeed! He wants to bless you, and He will give you a way to escape in tempting times, just like He promised He would: "No temptation has overtaken you except what is common to mankind. And God is faithful; he will not let you be tempted beyond what you can bear. But when you are tempted, he will also provide a way out so that you can endure it" (1 Corinthians 10:13). You have to be open and willing to accept and ac knowledge the way out and to follow it through, however. Remember, God is with you in everything: Jesus said, "And surely I am with you always, to the very end of the age" (Matthew 28:20b). This confirms that in everything you do, in everything you face, and during good times and challenging situations, He is there.

Sexual immorality has become incorporated into every aspect of our lives, so we can become desensitized to it even occurring. For example, a woman might be in the early stages of a relationship and the urges and desire may start to take over so the next seemingly normal step is to have sex. This may be the societal norm, but it is spiritually abnormal. God makes it clear that we are to be holy because His Holy Spirit cannot reside in immorality. This is not intended to imply that the occasional immoral offense separates you from God but that you will see the closeness you have with the Father start to dwindle if you repeatedly engage in ungodly behavior—not because He wants to leave you, but because you are leaving Him. Your focus becomes satisfying flesh and idolization rather than pleasing God. God gives you His word, in Hebrews 13:5, that He will never leave you or forsake you. This is where you step up in faith and realize that God is here to help as you rely on Him and not the world: "The Lord is my helper; I will not fear; what can man do to me?" (Hebrews 13:6).

Did you know that thinking about engaging in premarital sex is a sin? Desiring or experiencing lust for someone other than your husband is also a sin. This is how it starts: The thoughts come, you think about how good it was with a former lover or how good it would be with your new friend or man in your life, and you justify why it would be OK to be with that friend or man in your life. Although those thoughts may seem harmless, they are planting seeds that can produce an immoral action. You start contemplating the idea of having sex, and you begin to justify how meeting someone for drinks or to hang out poses no threat or risk. Next, you start thinking about what you will wear and convince yourself that the night is going to be just a fun night out. Deep down, however, you know the potential to have sex is there and that if the opportunity presents itself, you will go with it.

> It is God's will that you should be sanctified: that you should avoid sexual immorality; that each of you should learn to control your own body in a way that is holy and honorable, not in passionate lust like the pagans, who do not know God; and that in this matter no one should wrong or take advantage of a brother or sister. The Lord will punish all those who commit such sins, as we told you and warned you before. For God did not call us to be impure, but to live a holy life. Therefore, anyone who rejects this instruction does not reject a

human being but God, the very God who gives you his Holy Spirit. (1 Thessalonians 4:3–8)

Are you willing to reject God and your faith in God for moments or hours of pleasure by giving in to the adversary's plans to destroy your relationship with the Father? Sex is one area in which the adversary has succeeded in harming and/or destroying people's lives and families. Adulterous affairs are common-place in marriages, and premarital sex can lead to aborted or unwanted children, incurable diseases, single-parent homes, and children without an integral support system.

The result of sexual immorality is scary, but not scary enough to make most people stop engaging in the behavior. That may be because we know God is a graceful, merciful, and forgiving God and that once there is confession and repentance, He will forgive us and move on without a second thought to our sin. Or maybe it is because the validity of such indiscretion is so ingrained in our culture that we just go with the flow. Or it could be because we simply do not know what God says about the purity of our temple. Maintaining the purity of your spirit does not mean waiting ninety days, following the three-month rule; it means not having premarital sex or engaging in sexually immoral actions at all.

It is hard to wait (based on statistics stating that 95 percent of Americans have premarital sex) until you are married to have sex, but it is not impossible. God is extremely clear on His disdain for defiling the temple where He resides, as 1 Corinthians 6:9–10 hits home: "Or do you not know that wrongdoers will not inherit the kingdom of God? Do not be deceived: Neither the sexually immoral nor idolaters nor adulterers nor men who have sex with men nor thieves nor the greedy nor drunkards nor slanderers nor swindlers will inherit the kingdom of God." Revelation 21:8 adds, "But the cowardly, the unbelieving, the vile, the murderers, the sexually immoral, those who practice magic arts, the idolaters and all liars—they will be consigned to the fiery lake of burning sulfur. This is the second death." Terrifying, right? Compromising our sexual moral ethics is as common as breathing, but you can be victorious over sexual immorality!

Sexually immoral acts include viewing pornography, being unfaithful, and being lustful. People often wonder if watching pornography is a sin, because the Bible does not specifically say. Allow me to clear this up once and for all with a resounding yes! Observing pornographic media is a sin because it goes against God's instruction for you to be holy and faithful. The New Living Translation of 2 Peter 2:14 says, "They commit adultery with their eyes, and their desire for sin is never satisfied. They lure unstable people into sin, and they are well trained in greed. They live under God's curse." If your man is encouraging premarital sex or induces you to engage in premarital pornographic texting, he is not of God. If you engage in these activities, it is truly time for you to know God by reading and meditating on His Word, spending time with Him daily in prayer or talking with Him, and letting Him know how you feel and what is on your mind.

Most single women have that carnal urge or fleshly desire to engage in sexual intercourse with their man or a friend, but the key is to figure out ahead of time what to do when the urge arises and a situation to "get some" presents itself. You know it is coming, so what are you going to do? I will be honest: I did not think I would have to worry about who I would have sex with again once I met the man who would become my fiancé; I just knew he would be the one for the rest of my life, and I was perfectly fine with that. As a matter of fact, I found joy in knowing that I would be with only one person for the rest of my life! Unfortunately, he did not share my sentiments, so, two years after our last sexual encounter, I was struggling. I was going through my electronic phone book, thinking of who I could call to satisfy that carnal desire. When I found "the one," I called him, invited him to dinner, and then realized what a terrible idea it was. Though my body screamed, "Do it!" my spirit whispered, "You can't do this, Nicole." I could not bring myself to have casual sex and I canceled the dinner.

So how did I stop myself from engaging in ungodly and inappropriate behavior?

- **I took time to think about my actions.** When you have time to think clearly with your mind and not your libido, you make sound decisions.

- **My spirit condemned me.** God will let you know that what you are doing is wrong, and your spirit will speak to you against the actions you are going to take. I listened to it instead of ignoring it.

- **I realized that after two years of no sex, I did not want to give such a sacred and emotional gift to this person.** Ask yourself if the person is really worth you giving away a significant part of your spirit and soul to. (The answer is no because he is not your husband.)

Verses 3–5 of 1 Thessalonians says, "It is God's will that you should be sanctified: that you should avoid sexual immorality; that each of you should learn to control your own body in a way that is holy and honorable, not in passionate lust like the pagans, who do not know God." There are times when the spirit of lust comes upon you with such an overwhelming force that you want desperately to call up someone to have sex before you implode (or explode). But do not. You are able to refrain because of the Holy Spirit within and because you understand what you are doing to your body and spirit and to our Father. When we put the urge in those terms, the thought should really affect the decision that we make. That decision should be to honor our Father and to love ourselves. When these moments come upon us, we can follow a series of steps that can help us overcome the adversarial temptations.

## Read the Scriptures

It is critical to put on the armor of God daily so you can stand against the destructive plan of the devil to ruin you. Below are a few Scriptures that should give you strength as you meditate and focus on God's Word.

a.   "For our struggle is not against flesh and blood, but against the rulers, against the authorities, against the powers of this dark world and against the spiritual forces of evil in the heavenly realms." (Ephesians 6:12)

b.   "Love must be sincere. Hate what is evil; cling to what is good." (Romans 12:9)

c.   "He gives strength to the weary and increases the power of the weak." (Isaiah 40:29)

d.   "One day Jesus said to His disciples, 'There will always be temptations to sin, but what sorrow awaits the person who does the tempting!'" (Luke 17:1)

e.   "The Lord will fight for you; you need only to be still." (Exodus 14:14)

f.   "Put to death therefore what is earthly in you: sexual immorality, impurity, passion, evil desire, and covetousness, which is idolatry." (Colossians 3:5)

g.   "Be devoted to one another in love. Honor one another above yourselves." (Romans 12:10)

## Remember What You Are Doing to Your Body, Your Spirit, and Your Father

First Corinthians 6:19–20 reminds us: "Do you not know that your bodies are temples of the Holy Spirit, who is in you, whom you have received from God?

You are not your own; you were bought at a price (the price of His Son). Therefore honor God with your bodies." Once you are born again, the Holy Spirit dwells within and your body belongs to God. God gave His only Son as payment for you, for your sins to be washed away, for forgiveness, for life, and for love. He gave His only Son to save you because He knew you could not save yourself. With the death of His Son came the indwelling of the Holy Spirit in you, to help you and guide you. When you make decisions that defile your body, you are defiling God. He forgives you and washes your sins away, but because He lives within you, you hurt and disappoint Him when you knowingly engage in an activity that he detests, because you are making a conscious decision to go directly against God and the price He paid for you to be here. Remember to give yourself time to think about your actions. When you have time to think clearly with your heart and mind instead of your libido, you make sound decisions.

## Pray

Prayer changes things, really! God wants you to come to Him and tell Him how you feel. He wants to know that you consider Him to be a friend and that you know He is there for you in your times of need and weakness. God wants to know that you trust Him and will turn to Him for help instead of turning to someone who is leading you away from Him. God promises to hear you and not turn His back on you when you come to Him with an open heart. Jeremiah 29:12–13 says, "'Then you will call on Me and come and pray to Me, and I will listen to you. You will seek Me and find Me when you seek Me with all your heart. I will be found by you,' declares the Lord, 'and will bring you back from captivity.'"

These are God's words, and His Word is always true. He promises that He will be accessible to you when you come to Him. He will bring you back from sinful ways. He will bring you back from weakness and the spirit of lust, but you have to take the first step. Just as you should be looking for action from the guys you date to see if they are serious about you, God looks for action from you. He is not satisfied with words; anyone can say, "I am not going to have sex," but it takes a woman who puts God first to abstain from sex. Remember, your spirit will condemn you when you consider sinning. God will let you know that what you are doing is wrong, and your spirit will speak to you against the actions you are going to take. You must listen to your spirit instead of ignoring it.

## Don't Make or Accept Calls from Potential Sex Partners

Speaking with a potential sexual partner during a period of lust will only increase your chances of having sex. Staying clear of communication and contact with a potential sex partner will strengthen your chances of staying focused and staying in the will of God. Remove the temptation and multiply success.

## Ask Yourself: "Is This Person Worth Me Losing My Dignity and Self-Respect?"

I asked myself, "Is it worth me giving in to the devil's plan to try to destroy me and my relationship with God?" I realized that after two years of no sex, I was not willing to give away a sacred and emotional gift anymore! I would not allow the adversary to encourage my downward spiral of lust while losing my dignity.

Is this person really worth a significant part of your spirit and soul?

## Realize What Is Truly Happening

A battle is being fought in the spirit realm, and satan is trying to destroy you. Realize that the spirit of lust is of satan; all he wants to do is ruin you and your relationship with your loving Father: "The thief comes only to steal and kill and destroy; I have come that they may have life, and have it to the full" (John 10:10). Should you let him succeed?

When you get the urge and feel like you must have sex, that is the devil working to get you to rule over you. When this happens, it is time to power up your spirit. Satan does not care about you or your sex life, but he does care about getting you to go against God—the God who gave you life, sacrificed His only Son for you, healed your family member of disease, and provides you shelter and food. What will you do? Romans 8:38–39 says that nothing can separate you from the love of God—no power or principality, not even death. This is great news! It means you won't let satan win, because you have already won—Jesus has ensured it!

## Prepare and Plan for the Inevitable

Be strong and courageous. Say no to the late-night call. Let your friends with benefits know that their benefit package has been revoked!

The moment will present itself when you will be asked to be the other half of a late-night rendezvous. Make your potential partners aware of your decision before that moment arises. Make a list of the potential partners and let them know via phone call, text message, or e-mail that God has moved you from the worldly living that once consumed you and into godly living that now overwhelmingly satiates you with peace, joy, and a desire to make decisions that please Him and, as such, you will be unavailable to participate in sexual encounters.

## Call a Godly Girlfriend You Trust Who Can Talk You Down

Having a wise and trusted confidant who understands the importance of doing the right thing is a critical piece to helping you through a tempting period. It is essential that she not only has the qualities of a godly woman but also is someone you respect and whose advice you will heed. Do not call the girlfriend who tells you to give in to temptation and worry about the consequences later! Speak with the one who wants the best for you always and knows that that sometimes means denying flesh for the sake of spirit.

## Helpful Scriptures

"Finally, be strong in the Lord and in His mighty power. Put on the full armor of God, so that you can take your stand against the devil's schemes. For our struggle is not against flesh and blood, but against the rulers, against the authorities, against the powers of this dark world and against the spiritual forces of evil in the heavenly realms." (Ephesians 6:10–12)

"And pray in the Spirit on all occasions with all kinds of prayers and requests." (Ephesians 6:18) [This means that God wants you to pray about everything! Nothing is too small to bring to Him. He longs and desires for you to talk with Him and pray about your family, health, and, yes, even sex.]

## Activity

 Consider and finish the following thoughts.

When my flesh is tempted, the first step I will take is:

_____

_____

_____

_____

_____

This step will help me because:

_____

_____

_____

_____

_____

The Scripture that speaks to me most is:

_____

_____

_____

_____

I will also call this godly woman or prayer partner to support me in my moments of weakness.

_____

_____

## Prayers

<u>My Prayer</u>

Lord, I love You, and I thank You for the changes you are making in me. I repent of my sins. I confess that I have ignored Your will for my life and engaged in sexual activity. I lived in the world and followed the world. But now I live in You and in Your Word. I thank You for forgiving me of these transgressions and for making me better. I thank You for Your strength to overcome the temptations that will surely follow me on this walk to do better. I am grateful that by Jesus' stripes, I am healed. Thank You for being a God of renewal and forgiveness. I love You, Lord. In Jesus' name. Amen.

<u>Praise Report</u>!

Thank You, God, that I made it through! I triumphed over the trap set for me by the devil, who is always working on destroying me. I feel close to you and am grateful that I chose to walk in love and to honor You and myself. Thank You, Jesus, for the victory and I pray that you continue to give me the strength I need to overcome future temptations. I love You Lord and I pray these things in Jesus' name. Amen.

[Enjoy your victory; you did an awesome job! God is so proud of you, and so am I!]

<u>Prayer Request and Future Praise Report</u>!

Lord, I slipped. I did not follow the plan because my flesh got the better of me. I repent and ask for forgiveness. Thank You for forgiving me. I am ready to move forward and to focus on doing better. I need Your help; only You can help me through this. Denying my flesh and abstaining is more difficult than I thought, Lord, but I know that I am more than a conqueror and have the power of

Almighty Jesus within me. I will keep praying and will meditate on the Scripture and call my prayer partner for support. Thank You for another chance and for not leaving me as I go through this process. I love You. In Jesus' name I pray. Amen.

# 11

# SELF-LOVE AND ELEVATION

*There is no fear in love.*

—1 John 4:18a

## Waiting Is Self-love

*T*he topic of sex is delicate, and it is important to me that you know that this section is not meant to judge anyone who has premarital sex but to share what God says about it, how He feels about it, and what He will do about it. The good news is that because He is a forgiving God, He forgives our sins: "If we confess our sins, he is faithful and just and will forgive us our sins and purify us from all unrighteousness" (1 John 1:9). Being forgiven does not necessarily mean we walk away without our sin being addressed, but it does mean we become new in Him.

I have written a lot about love: being loved, loving God, and loving others. The same rules apply to loving God and loving yourself. When you show that you love God through the sacrifice of submission and obedience to Him, you are demonstrating self-love. Do you love yourself enough to wait? You now know with 100 percent certainty that any form of sexual activity is to be done with your husband. I have fallen short of this command, and perhaps you have too, but I am no longer allowing the devil to rule my decisions and me. I have made it known through my words and my actions that I am not going to have premarital sex. I have rejected offers, and I simply do not answer the phone or respond to text messages from anyone whose intentions are not pure. Answering those calls or texts leaves the door open for the two of you to connect, and if you respond to his message, even if to say no, he still thinks he has an opening.

When an opportunity arises to engage in a sexual encounter, consider how you feel when you have to leave someone's bed after a sex-only encounter because that was all you wanted, or to have someone leave your bed because you got what you needed. Think about how you would feel after staying in the bed with someone simply because you felt you needed that closeness. What you are truly longing for is a better relationship with our heavenly Father and to grow closer to Him. To be honest, the pleasure you received for an hour or two is not worth the condemnation you feel knowing that your heavenly Father is hurt and that you betrayed Him. It is just not worth it.

 **Red Flag:** If the word of your boyfriend is contrary to the Word of God, it's time to get out of the relationship.

When that lust demon rears its ugly head, I turn to Scripture, turn on Joel Osteen, or listen to messages from my pastor, Bishop Walter Thomas. I am reminded of the methods the devil uses and the traps he sets for us to fail. He knows where we are weak and exploits it. Let God be made strong where you are weak, and give God the glory when you send satan packing! Remember, God has a man, not a boy, for you. When you have sex, it will be with someone who cares deeply for you, someone who shows love by being kind and by putting you above himself, and he will be your husband. God has a man for you who is compassionate, slow to anger, and not mentally, physically, or emotionally abusive. Knowing this is true, I find myself encouraged and patiently waiting for God to do what He does best—rule my life!

Did you know that as a wife, your rewarding and pleasurable responsibility is to satisfy all of those sexy and sensual desires your husband has—and for your husband to satisfy yours? Thinking about making love with a man who loves me and is committed to both God and me is the definition of sexy. I cannot wait to get married and have sex with my husband—the *man*! I cannot wait to pleasure him and for us to enjoy each other and share those sensual, passionate, sexy and freaky moments! I am excited to know that the Lord is in charge and is going to take care of my needs.

I know without a doubt that God will send the person to me when we are both ready. I also know that He will send the right man for you when you are ready—so do not prolong the arrival of the amazing man God has created just for you. Do the right thing and be blessed now! Get excited about connecting with your husband on the most intense level instead of connecting with boys you have dated. Get excited about being with a man who honors and respects you—the man who knows and acts like he was made in the image of God.

You should be excited about being with a faithful man rather than a Cheater; a protector rather than a Bully; one who freely gives and takes care of you, rather than a User; one who can be honest and genuine rather than a Coward. Are you excited about having a man who makes you his priority and whom you can count on when times are tough? Are you ready to embrace the man who is the encourager and supporter, not the one who puts you down and makes you feel sad or bad about yourself? If you are excited, now is the time to stop crawling in and out of bed with boys who do not deserve you. They do not deserve to receive a part of you that is so sensitive and emotional. They do not deserve that part of your spirit. Remember, God says when you defile your body with sex, you are defiling Him. He does not deserve it and neither do you. Love yourself, enrich your self-worth, and save yourself from condemnation by waiting until you say, "I do," to *your man.*

When I look back, I see that I messed up on many levels with my former fiancé, including having premarital sex, living together while we were only engaged, and honoring him and his worldly ways over the word of God. Red flag, ladies: If the word of your boyfriend is contrary to the Word of God, it is time to get out of the relationship. I was not right. What I did was immoral and against God. But I am better now. I know better and do better, and I want the same for you. I am not looking back at the mistakes I made but am moving forward to be who God has called me to be.

It is important that you know that any boy who tells you to do things that are contrary to the Word of God is doing things that are contrary to a loving relationship with you, and that should not be tolerated. For example, while my former fiancé was encouraging me to move in with him, which was sinful and inappropriate, he was cheating on me; he was collecting the phone numbers of other women and engaging in other immoral acts. He was doing things with other women that were supposed to be special and exclusive between the two of us. Now is the time to say no to the boys and yes to whom God has for you. Say it out loud: "God, I am done with the boys. I say *no* to the boys, and I say *yes* to You and to the man You have for me! Thank You, God, for not giving up on me and for bringing me to this point of doing better and being better."

Sex before marriage and sex with the wrong person—the person not intended for you by God—can create challenging situations for both parties involved. Let's look at the biblical story of King David (2 Samuel 11). Just seeing Bathsheba bathing sent David into such a spiral of lust that he sent some of his people to bring her to him for the purpose of sex. David succumbing to the lust demon caused a horrific chain of events:

- David had sex with another man's wife.

- David fathered a child through the affair.

- David had Uriah, Bathsheba's husband, killed.

- The son of David and Bathsheba died.

- David was publicly humiliated when the Lord had his wives given to his closest associate for everyone to see.

Samson (Judges 14–16) is another biblical figure who gave in to lust. Beautiful women were his weakness, his Achilles' heel. He married a Philistine woman. Keep in mind, he had not spoken with her or courted her to determine if a mutual chemistry extended beyond the physical; he married her solely because of her beauty. He did not know anything about her, except that she was fine. For him, that was enough. The book of Judges goes on to tell us that she betrayed him to the Philistines. The next time the Bible mentions Samson with a woman is with a prostitute in Gaza, and the final mention is of him falling in love with Delilah. Through Scripture, we are able to learn that Samson enjoyed beautiful women but that the relationships lacked necessary components: love, loyalty, and a moral compass. Because these essentials were missing, the women were able to make Samson do things he did not want to do—like share the source of his strength or the answer to a riddle. It is critical that you do not lie with just anybody for worldly reasons (he is cute, or he can give you something you want), especially because having sex with someone for such worldly reasons goes against the foundation of a healthy relationship and you being a godly woman.

One girlfriend of mine dated the pastor of a church. About six months into their relationship, they started having sex. When they had started dating, she had shared that she felt relief because, since he was a pastor, sex would not enter their relationship…or so she thought. When he eventually pursued a sexual relationship with her, she thought it must be okay because he was the leader of the church, responsible for saving souls, and helped people know Christ. She phoned me after convincing herself that because he had been handpicked by God and had been charged to be better, premarital sex must be okay…right? *Wrong!* It was not okay. Pastor or not, he is a man, and he, like other men, is carnal and driven by flesh. The devil knows what traps to set and how to set you up for failure. I pray this book helps you to discern situations that are satan traps and to steer clear of them. Remember, if your man does not honor you or love you, if he uses and/or abuses you, if he pretends to be someone he is not and his words do not match his actions, he is not for you and is not the man God wants for you.

In Part III, we looked at the importance of God abiding in your man. When someone abides in you, that is as close as someone can get to you. A sexual encounter is as close as someone can be with you. Remember, God tells us that we are His, we are not our own, and when you defile your temple, you are defiling

Him. When you engage in sexual activity, it should only be in a time of love when the two of you are married. When you marry, the second-closest relationship you will ever have is created, and it is at this time that the two of you will become one flesh; Matthew 19:4–5 says, "And he answered and said, 'Have you not read that he who created them from the beginning made them male and female, and said, "for this reason a man shall leave his father and mother and be joined to his wife, and the two shall become one flesh"?'"

God wants you to experience His amazing blessing and to receive all that He has for you. He takes the time to warn you to "flee from sexual immorality" in 1 Corinthians 6:18. True men of God consider sexual morality an important piece of the big marriage picture. A godly man understands that "charm is deceptive, and beauty is fleeting; but a woman who fears the Lord is to be praised" (Proverbs 31:30). Being promiscuous or unfaithful or having premarital sex carries a higher public burden for women than it does for men, as it did even in biblical times. John 8:3 shares how the Pharisees brought a woman who was caught committing adultery for stoning—but where was the man? If she was caught in the act, surely the man was with her, but the Pharisees seemingly let him go because adultery was more egregious for the woman to commit than for the man.

Chapter 10 highlighted the wisdom of steering clear of a man who encourages you or tempts you to have sex. Joseph is a good example of such a man, in Genesis 39:7–12: King Potiphar's wife sexually pursued Joseph, and he consistently denied her persistent advances. Joseph trusted and had faith in the Father; he was not going to let physical enjoyment take precedence over God's will. He also would not give in to a woman he recognized as lacking moral character. If she could be this treacherous and not give two thoughts about her obligation to honoring God, she could indeed be diabolical in other areas of her life, which she proved to be. After many unsuccessful attempts of coercing, bullying, and seducing Joseph, the queen could not move him to sleep with her, so she lied to her husband, King Potiphar, telling him that Joseph had raped her.

Not all men will go to the extremes that King Potiphar's wife did, but if a man regularly encourages or tempts you to have premarital sex, it is a sign that he is not ready to be the godly man for you.

## Being the Other Woman

Another category of sexual immorality that can hinder self-love is having sex with a married man. God speaks specifically to dishonoring the sanctity of marriage, just as He shuns premarital sex, fornication, and lust. In Leviticus 20:10,

God told Moses, "If a man commits adultery with another man's wife—with the wife of his neighbor—both the adulterer and the adulteress are to be put to death." I am picking up on a pattern here: everything sexually immoral ends in death. The good news is that once you repent, renew your mind and flee from the sexually immoral, you do not have to worry about death, because God gave you a way of escape and His Name is Jesus! The death of Jesus became the death for your sins and eternal life for you. Recall the adulteress whom the Pharisees brought to be stoned, and understand that she was not condemned to death because the Lord gave her an opportunity to be free and told her to "go and leave your life of sin" (John 8:11).

If you make the poor decision to engage in adulterous activity with a married man, I ask that you think about the wife, the child of God, to whom you are causing harm. She is your sister in Christ and deserves to be honored and respected, if not by her husband, then at least by her sister. You have got to have your sister's back. Someone has to look out for the women, and it could be that God has placed you in front of this husband to be an ambassador of Christ for his wife. Even though you may have never met her, you have an opportunity to protect her and love her. Do not choose to be a part of the reason for emotional and mental harm and perhaps a broken family. Think about how you would feel if you found out that your husband, fiancé, or boyfriend was cheating. If you have not experienced it, praise the Lord! If you have, you know it is the most devastating blow to your mental and emotional health. I have been the fiancée of a cheating man and even knew the woman he cheated with, and it was the worst hurt I had ever experienced. Those immoral actions had such an injurious effect on me that I required counseling as part of my healing process. Intentionally causing harm to a married couple is harmful for everyone involved, including those directly and indirectly involved.

A dear friend of mine, Holly, whom I have known for more than twenty years, had an affair with a married man, John. She started the relationship unaware that he was married (she had asked, but he had denied it). They lived in different states, but they communicated daily through phone calls, FaceTime, and texts. They would see each other a couple of times a month at her house or a hotel. She finally inquired about coming to his house for the weekend and received a lot of pushback. She continued to bring it up over the next couple of weeks until he finally broke down and said he was married. She instantly ended the relationship and cut off all communication with him.

She thought that was the end of the story, but then came the adversary. As time progressed, she missed John. She no longer had her partner, her friend whom she could talk with after a long day, share great news with, meet for the special midweek date, or feel that special closeness she had with him. He was familiar, and she was comfortable with him. She had not dated anyone new and had no desire to do so. She just could not get John out of her mind. She called me to discuss her feelings, but despite my wise advice, she allowed her thoughts and emotions to guide her actions and rekindled their relationship. She called him, and they picked up right where they left off. She was now *knowingly* the other woman.

There was just something about John that allowed Holly to throw her moral compass out the window. For as long as I have known Holly, she has always had a fervent disdain for the unfaithful, so what happened over the course of the past few years that had her playing an active role in this adulterous affair? John was her safe place and provided some seemingly absent components to her life. She enjoyed having a friend and a lover. She talked a lot about their ability to make each other laugh and how they were able to make each other feel better after a tough day. She needed intimacy and companionship. Her friend and lover had returned. She enjoyed having that lonely void filled with conversations and secret hotel meetings even though they left her waking up by herself because he returned home to his wife. While they were apart, she had longed to have an emotional and physical connection and was accustomed to having it.

Holly and I had discussions at length about the situation and about her walking away. She acknowledged, with teary eyes, that she was ashamed of her actions and had been trying for months to end it. A stronghold prevented her from severing her ties to him. She even mentioned that she and John had had long talks about their role as Christians and about how they could not keep living in sin. He wanted to do right by his wife, and Holly wanted to do right by God.

Holly and John ended their affair several times but found the temptation and attraction more difficult to overcome each time. On average, they would resume communication and the affair within two weeks of ending it. This happened over and over again.

On their last date night, they both agreed that they had to be strong, stay prayed up, and ask the Lord to help them fight the temptation to see and speak with each other. More than three months later, they still have not communicated. Holly calls me when she feels the urge to reach out to him, and I talk her down as we focus on the love of Jesus and His power. She has her moments of weakness but fights the temptation just to "check on him and say hi" by putting love first. One of her daily meditations is "love does no harm to a neighbor," and she knows that contacting him is not loving and causes harm to her neighbors.

Do you tolerate cheating, or is it a relationship breaker? I used to always say that a man cheating on me would be a relationship breaker, but that changed when I was engaged. Though my fiancé cheated on me, I felt that with the power of God, he could be the man he proclaimed to be and could end his affairs. I believed he would end the affairs because he said he would, and I believed God would keep our relationship together. God cannot keep together what He knows needs to be separated, however.

God cherishes all covenants, especially the covenant of marriage, with tremendous value. Hebrews 13:4 says, "Let marriage be held in honor among all, and let the marriage bed be undefiled, for God will judge the sexually immoral and adulterous." When you sleep with another woman's husband, it is a clear indication that you do not honor God or the godly bond of marriage. God made covenants to be everlasting and unbreakable commitments to be held in the highest esteem and reverence. What would have happened if God had broken His covenant with Abraham, Noah, or David? Though marriage is not listed as one of God's primary covenants (Adamic, Abrahamic, Noahic, Davidic, Mosaic, Palestinian, and New), it is a covenant and does carry the terms of a covenant as a lifelong commitment to unconditionally love and honor your spouse. Marriage is a mutually beneficial relationship in which each party is greatly concerned with the well-being of and has a genuine desire to be a blessing to the other, which is confirmed by the oath that each party vows to uphold. This is not to say that the expectation should be a perfect marriage, because that is simply not realistic, but it does mean that the intention you have for the other person should be pure and selfless. Though husband and wife will disagree, make mistakes, say hurtful things, and so on, the covenant remains intact.

## The Game Changer

Women (and men, too) are known for playing their share of games in relationships. Some women believe they are justified in playing games when they do not receive a response they were hoping for, or sometimes they play games to get their man's attention, make him jealous, make him sad, or even make him angry because anger will at least show that he cares, right? This is what the world has led us to believe for centuries. I cannot turn on my television without seeing someone playing, plotting, or scheming against his or her significant other. God says to always take the high road, be open, be honest, and love. Love does not invent scenarios in which anger, jealousy, lust, and/or fear are purposely created. Remember, love builds up and does not tear down.

My client Diane is a very kind and compassionate individual who has a genuine desire to help people. Listening to her in weekly sessions sheds a lot of light onto who she is. She knows how to set boundaries in relationships and does not take any wooden nickels, but she knows how to get what she wants with an uncanny ability to manipulate a man's behavior. She plays the relationship game to win on every level by controlling the narrative and outcome. Diane is currently planning her wedding to her long-term on-and-off boyfriend, Evan. During the dating phase, she would purposely get him to feel angry, fearful of losing her, and even jealous. She believed such manipulation could lead to an engagement ring.

When I delved more deeply with Diane, I realized that her desire to control his actions gave her a feeling of safety and security: If she knew what was going to happen, she felt good and was able to continue in the relationship. The unknown was what Diane feared; not knowing what was going to happen or what Evan's response would be was too much for her to handle. After many years of playing the game, she had gotten the ring and was officially engaged to Evan. After a few months of wearing the ring she had worked so hard for, however, Diane realized she did not want to marry Evan.

When God is involved in your life and the relationship, you, like Diane, realize that playing games is substandard for you as His daughter and that if games are required to get the ring, this may not be the relationship for you and it is probably time for prayer and self-reflection.

Women have also been led to believe that showing love and kindness is a sign of weakness, but it is simply not true. Not only is Jesus love—while on Earth, He lived a life showering people with love—but He remains the strongest, most powerful man ever because He shared and showed love (and continues to do so). His strength and power were demonstrated in His selfless acts that promoted others. Those who know Jesus know there is nothing weak about Him. And because He is perfect, He would not instruct anyone to do anything that would cause your demise. The adversary, however, will and does. If your man is unwilling to accept and receive your love and kindness as intended by the Spirit, he is probably not the one for you. God wants both people involved to be kind, loving, open, and honest. He is not looking for players of the game; He wants game changers.

## Helpful Scriptures

"For the LORD detests the perverse but takes the upright into his confidence." (Proverbs 3:32)

"As a result, we are no longer to be children, tossed here and there by waves and carried about by every wind of doctrine, by the trickery of men, by craftiness in deceitful scheming; but speaking the truth in love, we are to grow up in all *aspects* into Him who is the head, *even* Christ, from whom the whole body, being fitted and held together by what every joint supplies, according to the proper working of each individual part, causes the growth of the body for the building up of itself in love." (Ephesians 4:14–16)

"You were bought at a price. Therefore honor God with your bodies." (1 Corinthians 6:20)

"Flee the evil desires of youth and pursue righteousness, faith, love and peace, along with those who call on the Lord out of a pure heart." (2 Timothy 2:22)

"Do not lie to each other, since you have taken off your old self with its practices and have put on the new self, which is being renewed in knowledge in the image of its Creator." (Colossians 3:9–10)

## Activity

Have you ever been the other woman? What does it mean to you as a woman of God to fill this role? God says to love your neighbor as yourself; are you showing love to your neighbor, his wife, or yourself? Remember, when you honor and respect yourself, you are less likely to focus on a self-centered activity that places you on the path of satan's plan to kill, steal, and destroy.

_____

_____

_____

_____

_____

How do you think you would feel if you found out your man had the other woman? If you are the other woman, put yourself in his wife's shoes and explain how you feel about him having the other woman.

_____

_____

_____

_____

_____

If you have had or are having an affair with a married man, what are the reasons that you started the relationship and are continuing it?

_____

_____

_____

_____

_____

Have you found yourself playing games in your relationship to get what you want? If so, do you find that the games give you the desired results?

_____

_____

_____

_____

_____

After reading this chapter, do you feel it is necessary to continue to play games in a relationship to orchestrate your desired outcome? If so, explain.

_____

_____

_____

_____

_____

How do you think God feels about any games you may play? If you were having a one-on-one discussion with Him, what do you think He would tell you about your next steps as the other woman or as a player of the game?

_____

_____

_____

_____

_____

It is important to recognize that the adversary is using you to wreak havoc on not only yourself but also on the man, his wife, their household and children, your relationship with God, the relationship between your man and family, and your blessings. Keep in mind that God blesses obedience.

## Prayer

Heavenly Father, I come to Your throne boldly with thanksgiving and requests. I thank You for Your unfailing love and for never giving up on me. I pray that You rid me of anything that is not of You. Give me a clean heart and spirit, and allow my focus to be on You and my actions to be driven by Your love. I have not loved others as I should, as You have instructed, but today is a new day for me to start! I thank You for another chance and pray for your continued mercy and grace as I try to do better. Today and every day, I will power up with prayer and quiet time with You as You show me the way to go. I love You, Lord. In Jesus' name I pray. Amen.

# WHAT'S NEXT?

*So let's not get tired of doing what is good. At just the right time
we will reap a harvest of blessing if we don't give up.*

—Galatians 6:9

*A* s women of God, we all have the responsibility to power up and demonstrate His love in our lives. You have the privilege of being His representative on Earth with every word you speak and every step you take. You have been selected to demonstrate His love with everyone. He relies on you to be a beacon of light and hope for the hopeless and the faithless in a world that is regularly filled with darkness and despair. You, woman of God, have been called to defend, lead by example, and leave a loving legacy for the next generation.

## The DEAL (Defender, Example, And Legacy)

### DEFENDER

You are a Defender of women everywhere. (You should picture yourself in a cape at the top of a mountain; that is how I see it!) You have been charged to replace the negative image of worldly women with the loving image of godly women. If you are a woman of God, you have been charged to represent Him in every area, especially in relationships. The world's negative influence seems to have control in that area for now. When women see you stand tall in love and honoring God, yourself, and your man, you will see change happen, though it will take Defenders rising up all over to do what is right and pleasing to the Lord for that change to happen.

Being a Defender also includes protecting your inner circle. It is nonnegotiable that the people who have access to me and my daughter share the same godly mentality. People who do not share that mentality are not allowed to cross that protected threshold into our lives. I find that this is one area where people are very lax. It is extremely important to be cognizant of and to monitor the people you allow in your life, as it is integral to the well-being of both you and your family that your intimate circle is only filled with people with good spirits. The adversary is always at work and sends some people your way to get you off of your game and initiate your spiritual demise. If you think about it long enough, you will recall someone in your life whose main accomplishment was interfering with your Christian living. I am a firm believer of protecting your heart and spirit, where the Father dwells, as well as your physical home. Inviting people you do not know into your space could introduce unwanted feelings that penetrate your covered and protected home: depression, fear, anger, worry, and any other negative spirit.

Be wise to discern who is of God and who is not, and remember that it is okay to kick people out of your life who are contrary to God's planned purpose for you. In Matthew 21:12–13, Jesus kicks out the people who are defiling the temple: "Jesus entered the temple courts and drove out all who were buying and selling there. He overturned the tables of the money changers and the benches of those selling doves. 'It is written,' he said to them, '"My house will be called a house of prayer," but you are making it "a den of robbers."'" Just as Jesus protected the temple, He wants you to protect your temple and to rid yourself of those who are robbing you of your glorious destiny.

## EXAMPLE

You are the Example modeling—for your daughters, nieces, sisters, and the girls who observe you at the grocery store, in the mall, at the movies, and on dates—what a woman should be in relationships. What example is being set for the next generation of women? If girls and young women are forced to rely on the example set by the world, they are going to grow up living in a man-made darkness where the focus is self-pleasure. This unhealthy environment will promote the adversary to thrive as he seeks to destroy relationships with the Father, steal self-esteem, and kill the possibility of healthy relationships and marriages. We cannot allow this to take place. I believe that through everything we see taking place in the world, God is telling us to rise up and do what He has called us to do and be who He has called us to be. He wants us to share our faith and trust in Him to create positive change in the world; change starts with you and me.

I think about my young daughter before I make any decision. I do not parade men around her, and I speak about the love of God and what that means for her. Even my private actions include her, because I know that spirits exist and I do not want to introduce lustful or disobedient spirits into our lives or home. For example, I would not go out and engage in drunkenness or promiscuous activity, and I would not curse anyone out or do anything else that I would not want her to do, so my example also includes leading with a pure heart and spirit.

Every interaction she sees with me is loving and kind as well, as are the interactions she does not. She has observed that there are times in life when firmness and sternness are required, but never disrespect. In public places, like the park, zoo, mall, or restaurants, young girls and women see how I lovingly communicate with my daughter, even if she is being corrected, and take the time to inform me of what a great mother I am. Though I appreciate the compliment, I hope and pray that they will carry on the example to mothers and fathers who think it is necessary to curse their children out.

It is important to me that my daughter, niece, cousins, and other girls see a strong woman who leans on the Lord as she faces tumultuous challenges. They see that even when people intentionally do their best to bring me down, I call on the name of Jesus, and though they may knock me down, I get up. For example, for more than two years, one person's sole intention was to bring about my mental, emotional, financial, and spiritual demise, all while the person professed to be a Christian and a person of God. As the person came at me again and again with everything they had and knocked me down, I got up. But then the person noticed something: As evil tried harder and harder to take me out, I stopped being knocked down. What the adversary did not realize was that each blow he used to weaken my spirit made me stronger. Initially, I had privately cried out to the Lord with tears streaming down my face, but then had come the day when I wasn't crying any more but boldly declaring, "Bring it on; I'm ready!" That day ended the cycle of falling and getting back up and started the phase of bobbing and weaving as the Lord directed my steps to block what was coming my way. Through it all, I remained focused on God and on His promises to make it through and to overcome the attacks.

It's also important for me to set an example as a woman who takes pride in her appearance. Growing up, I cannot recall one instance of my mother leaving the house with her hair in curlers or tied up, or in clothing that was meant solely for the home. I believe I followed suit because my mother set that example. My daughter is a toddler, and even at this early phase in her life, she does not leave our home without being presentably attired and her hair nice and neat. Because I expect it of myself (and I want her to expect it of me too), I model that we have a standard to uphold regarding our outward image. As a representative of God, I hope to represent Him in action, speech, and appearance, and by honoring Him, I honor myself. I know that people are *always* looking and it is our responsibility, as people of God, to set good examples. It is important to think about the example you are setting and if it is something you would want to see your daughter mimic.

## LEGACY

A legacy is something that you give or leave to someone, or something someone inherits directly from you. I recall pledging Delta Sigma Theta Sorority, Inc., at Tennessee State. If a girl was a legacy, meaning her mother or sister belonged to the organization, it was certain that she would be admitted because of her legacy connection. The legacy you give someone can help her become the woman of God she is to be or can leave her struggling on the other end of the spectrum. What will be your legacy to the next generation of women—your daughter, your granddaughter, cousins twice removed, and young girls you do not even know who are affected by your actions?

The example you set today will help shape someone's tomorrow. I pray you will be an example of a Defender coming together with other Defenders to love and renounce the carnal norm of the world and that you represent God in speech and deed (because people are always watching). The legacy I want to leave for my daughter (and other girls) involves her having faith and trusting in the Lord for everything, being loving and respectful, knowing when it is time to stand up for important matters of principle and when it is time to let it go, and knowing that her smile goes a long way to make people feel comfortable and at ease. I pray that when the adversaries of life come knocking, she will know to turn to the Lord and trust Him because plotting and scheming to "win" will only result in a win for the adversary. She will know how to express herself, and because she has never heard me use an expletive, she will use her extensive vocabulary to effectively communicate and will reject the promptings of the adversary to practice ignorance. She will know that her power comes from the Lord and that she has His power within to accomplish anything: to fight through life's challenges, to stay strong in the Lord, and to avoid succumbing to the temptations of the world. She will know that by seeking God first, she will receive the desires of her heart. Last but not least, she will know that, when in doubt, the correct answer is always to love.

## Get Powered Up!

When you realize and accept that it is time to do better and be better, it is important that you ask God to teach you and show you better ways and help you interpret and incorporate His teachings into your everyday life through His grace. This includes loving yourself and being wise, having faith and trusting in the Lord, and honoring God by honoring yourself and your relationship.

God is very clear about who He is and who He expects you to be; this book has revealed many of those expectations. When we decide to live lives pleasing to others and not to God, the results are not good:

- Potential negative effects when children are removed from a loving and balanced two-parent household and forced into a single-parent home

- Marriages ending in bitter and costly divorce battles

- Individuals distancing themselves from relationships with God

- The demise of the nuclear family because of our sinful ways

- People taking the lives of our young children in schools and other public places that were once considered safe

There are many spirits in the spirit realm. They can be spirits of the adversary, such as the spirits of deceit, shame, depression, lust, and evil, or spirits from our Father, which include love, integrity, humility, and truth. You must decide which side of the chasm you will live your life: Will you live for satan or for God? Will you live a life to satisfy yourself and the world, or will you make decisions that will glorify and honor God?

As you think about your life and how you will lead it, remember that God's Word is true and He created it so we can all do better and be better. The journey will be challenging, but it is possible. God is waiting for you right now to make the best decision to follow Him and to be the godly woman He called you to be before you were born. God transforms. He will change your heart and you will see a distinct difference between the renewed you and the former you. Get ready for the change and get powered up!

## Helpful Scriptures

"All Scripture is God-breathed and is useful for teaching, rebuking, correcting and training in righteousness so that the servant of God may be thoroughly equipped for every good work." (2 Timothy 3:16–17)

"As obedient children, do not conform to the evil desires you had when you lived in ignorance. But just as He who called you holy, so be holy in all you do." (1 Peter 1:14–15)

"Do not conform to the pattern of this world, but be transformed by the renewing of your mind. Then you will be able to test and approve what God's will is—his good, pleasing and perfect will." (Romans 12:2)

"There was the true Light which, coming into the world, enlightens every man. He was in the world, and the world was made through Him, and the world did not know Him. He came to His own, and those who were His own did not receive Him. But as many as received Him, to them He gave the right to become children of God, *even* to those who believe in His name, who were born, not of blood nor of the will of the flesh nor of the will of man, but of God." (John 1:9–13)

"Whoever heeds discipline shows the way to life, but whoever ignores correction leads others astray." (Proverbs 10:17)

"Do your best to present yourself to God as one approved, a worker who does not need to be ashamed and who correctly handles the word of truth." (2 Timothy 2:15)

## Activity

What is your ideal legacy for the next generation? What will you do or what changes will you make to leave this legacy?

_____

_____

_____

_____

_____

## Prayer

 Call on the name of Jesus...Jesus...Jesus...feel the power in His name. Praise His name because He is worthy to be praised! As you pray, see yourself breaking the chain of the adversary. *Hallelujah. See yourself rising up in victory. Thank God that you have triumphed! Thank God that you are powered up with His loving Spirit to receive every amazing blessing He has for you.* Lord, thank You for loving me. You sacrificed everything for me, and it is time that I start making more of an effort to be who You have called me to be: a godly woman, a woman of God. I used to take that title lightly, but I realize it is time to power up and be that woman! I have, sometimes knowingly and unknowingly, blocked or delayed blessings by following the ways of the world and not You. As I continue to seek You, I pray that You speak to me, guide me, and give me the power and strength to resist the traps of the adversary. Please help me to be God-centered and not self-centered. As I focus on my future, I am going to make every effort to leave the legacy of a godly woman in everything I do for the next generation. I am powered up and ready to be used by You, and I am ready for the godly man You have created for me! In Jesus' name. Amen.

## Prayers, Notes, Thoughts,et.

# Prayers, Notes, Thoughts,et.

# Prayers, Notes, Thoughts,et.

# Prayers, Notes, Thoughts,et.

# Prayers, Notes, Thoughts, et.

# About the Author:

 Nicole Showell is the founder and president of the Showell Foundation, Inc. and The Showell Group. She brings more than 15 years of professional counseling experience to families, couples, and young people of all ages. Nicole is driven to facilitate positive change in the lives of people and communities. Her work has helped many people across the country, from high school students to executives to professional athletes. Her tireless effort to promote healthy living and a vibrant society rely heavily on her love for Jesus Christ and mastery of her counseling style. She focuses on building trusting relationships, developing healthy behaviors, and focusing on heart change that will inspire and promote transformation at the most important level. Nicole is passionate about her work, and is invested in helping people experience changed hearts and live better lives.

As an experienced and seasoned presenter and public speaker, Nicole is a recognized motivator who shares her own innovative concepts. Informed by her own life's story, she diligently works to enrich diverse groups and inspire renewed company passion. Through workshops, corporate coaching, individual and group counseling, Nicole helps employees and business leaders find and achieve a healthy and balanced lifestyle while expanding organizational output and growth.

Nicole received her Master of Arts in Counseling from Biblical Theological Seminary, and has received numerous awards, including being recognized as an Honorary Speaker from the Congressional Black Caucus. She is committed to investing in the lives of others to help improve their outlook about career, health, education and family. Nicole seeks to encourage and inspire others to pursue excellence in life by developing a healthy mind, body and spirit while changing hearts through love!™

CPSIA information can be obtained
at www.ICGtesting.com
Printed in the USA
BVHW041739221219
567507BV00011B/384/P